RELIGIOUS LIBERTY
AND
THE AMERICAN PRESIDENCY

1963
HERDER AND HERDER NEW YORK
232 Madison Avenue, New York 16, NY

Library of Congress Catalog Card Number: 63–9558
© 1963 Herder and Herder, Inc.
Printed in the United States of America

Religious Liberty
and
The American Presidency

A Study in Church-State Relations

PATRICIA BARRETT

HERDER AND HERDER

FOREWORD

IT may be fairly said, if only because it has been said often enough, that we Americans are somewhat prone to live the unexamined life, without great regard for Socrates' dictum that such a life is not worth leading. We get things done; we go on to the next things to be done. We are not much given to reflection on the thing done or on the mode of its doing in order to appraise the significance and style of our own achievements. For instance, we made a bit of political history in 1960 by electing a Catholic to the presidency. The margin was close; nonetheless, the history was made. A due measure of professional attention has been given to statistical analysis of the vote with a view to estimating the influence of the religious issue on it. On the other hand, little reflection has been devoted to the issue itself, to the reasons for its rise in the campaign, its manifold content, or the variant modes of its presentation. This kind of reflection, however, is seriously needed. The 1960 vote settled the question of whether a Catholic can be elected to the highest office in the land. But in the electoral process of settling this minor and narrow issue, a number of larger issues and some passions too came up and out, and they were not settled or stilled by the vote.

These issues and the passions antecedent or consequent to

them are still with us. The relation between religion and politics and between morality and law; the legitimate claims and rightful powers of religious communities, who are at war with one another on the plane of theology within the one body politic and whose climate must be one of civil peace; the reach of religious liberty in society, especially in the school, in relation to the legal implications of separation of church and state—these and cognate issues cannot be settled by the technique of the ballot box. In fact, they cannot be finally settled at all; they are inherent in the permanent public argument.

Here the merit and service of Mother Barrett's book appear. It is a summons to reflection on the past, on the electoral campaign of 1960; it is also a call to continuing public argument on the issues that the campaign revealed to be still burning, or at least smoking, among us. The book is excellent in every respect. It is the product of painstaking research, whose doing must have been a test of temper as well as of intelligence—of intelligence because most of the 1960 campaign literature on the religious issue was extremely confused, and of temper because much of it was the passionate sort of nonsense that tends to wake in the reader a weary impatience, if not some more incandescent sentiment. The serenity of Mother Barrett's study commands instant admiration. So too does her clear-sighted objectivity and the unerring insight with which she finds her way through the clashing confusions of the campaign argument to the heart of the issues involved. This is the outstanding value of the book: that it transposes the issues into a form of statement that makes them arguable. The author's own arguments are a model of reason and candor. They are presented forthrightly and with sturdy Catholic conviction; their presentation is also informed by the gentle spirit of civic friendship. Mother Barrett has made a major contribution to the substance of the public argument. She has also done the further service of setting its proper tone.

JOHN COURTNEY MURRAY, S.J.

Woodstock College
September, 1962

CONTENTS

INTRODUCTION

MATURITY requires control and something to be controlled. Political maturity implies a measure of control over the native forces of self-interest flexible enough to permit keen competition and orderly enough to prevent disruptive clashes. American democracy underwent a testing of its maturity in the 1960 campaign which ended with the election of the first Roman Catholic to the office of President. The strain of the experience was, in some measure, proportionate to the intensity of the anti-Catholicism abroad in the land. Although the depth of this feeling cannot be accurately assessed, its pervasiveness can be amply documented. There is, moreover, disconcerting evidence that its roots lie deep in a heritage of ignorance and misunderstanding of the meaning of American democracy and the nature and purposes of Roman Catholicism.

The aim of this book is, quite simply, to report and evaluate the campaign charges against Catholicism and indicate what they reveal of contemporary American attitudes regarding (1) the relationship of religion to politics, (2) the compatibility of Catholicism and American freedom, (3) trends in interfaith dialogue, and (4) the expanding dimensions of the whole problem of religious liberty. The precise subject matter is the religious issue in the 1960 presidential election. The primary concern is the substantive aspect of the "Catholic question"—

1

its implications for the American way of life and the future of the free society. It does not directly treat the statistical problem of the extent to which President Kennedy's religion helped or hurt his final vote tally. Neither does it deal immediately with the political strategy woven around the issue by the campaign managers on both sides.[1]

The chief reason for pursuing this election post-mortem is the curious fact that even though the alleged impossibility of electing a Catholic President has been proven false, the familiar charges against Catholicism are still very much alive. The target of attack has shifted from the President as symbol to certain Congressmen and churchmen accused of crude power plays for narrow sectarian purposes. Perhaps we need frequent reminding of the value of tension in a democracy and of the inevitable diversity of interests and of methods by which such a society achieves its ends. Dissenting opinions are not very popular in an age of conformism which sets a high premium on national unity. They are nonetheless indispensable to progress and to the authentic freedom which men today are claiming as a basic human right. The inner dynamics of a pluralist society are never finally mastered, especially as they apply to the coexistence of multiple religious groups within a single political unit, and thus call for continual reassessment of ultimate and proximate loyalties. Partners in this kind of enterprise face the bipolar danger of a timid emasculation of essential religious commitments on the one hand and, on the other, an intransigence which could push the nation into either

[1] Theodore H. White, *The Making of the President, 1960,* New York, Atheneum, 1961, pp. 106–109.

2

a costly vertical pluralism or a shackling monolithism at odds with our historical tradition.[2] An obvious approach to the dilemma would be to submit recurrent church-state problems to rational public argument which, if it cannot be expected to resolve differences, might at least promote understanding and contribute to viable and equitable accommodations. But rational public debate presupposes a degree of intellectual sophistication, patience, and emotional detachment uncongenial to the American ethos with its passion for vigorous action and quick and total solutions to vexing problems. At best, we can hope for some larger endorsement of the wisdom of such an approach.

The following pages draw attention to persistent underlying tensions which lend themselves to fruitful exploration or fatal exploitation. Many Americans thought that the worst extremes of bigotry and prejudice had been laid to rest alongside Al Smith's presidential aspirations in 1928. The record, however, shows that professional bigots were more active in 1960 than in 1928, and further, their "output was swamped by that of the more 'respectable' non-professional anti-Catholic. And the content of the bulk of the material published in 1960 was infinitely more sophisticated."[3] There were also many serious and sincere statements which raised legitimate questions about the suitability of a Catholic as President. These deserve considera-

[2] See David O. Moberg, "Religion and Society in the Netherlands and in America," *American Quarterly*, Summer, 1961, pp. 172–178; Gerhard Lenski, *The Religious Factor*, New York, Doubleday, 1961. The latter author indicates the drift in American society toward "compartmentalization."

[3] Arnold Forster, "No Religious Test Shall Be Required . . . ," *ADL Bulletin*, November, 1960, p. 2.

tion and response as much for the truth they contain as for the error they convey.

The primary sources for this study include the propaganda pieces circulated throughout the country during the protracted struggle, and the information and insights gained from personal interviews and correspondence with men and women directly or indirectly associated with the campaign. The most complete collection of items dealing with the religious issue is located at the headquarters of the Fair Campaign Practices Committee, 45 East 65th Street, New York. Along with the exhibits themselves, the Committee has in its files an excellent annotated bibliography of related material and sundry background publications.

Appendix A in this book contains (1) an annotated selection of significant campaign pieces, and (2) a selected list of books, articles, and other materials dealing with religion and the 1960 presidential election. Appendix B contains (1) the text of "A Statement by the National Conference of Citizens for Religious Freedom," Washington, D.C., September 7, 1960; (2) "A Statement on Religious Liberty in Relation to the 1960 Campaign," September 12, 1960, signed by 100 Protestant, Greek Orthodox, Roman Catholic, and Jewish churchmen and scholars; (3) the text of Senator John F. Kennedy's speech to the Greater Houston Ministerial Association, September 12, 1960; and (4) "A Statement on Religious Liberty by American Catholic Laymen," October, 1960. These statements provide significant clues to the major political and psychological forces at work during the historic campaign.

4

Of the many friends and associates to whom I am grateful for help and inspiration in carrying through this project, I owe special thanks to the following: Dr. John C. Bennett, dean of faculty at Union Theological Seminary; Mr. Virgil L. Border, director of the St. Louis Office of the National Conference of Christians and Jews (NCCJ); Mother Louise Callan, R.S.C.J., professor of history, Maryville College; Rev. Francis Canavan, S.J., associate editor of *America*; Dr. C. Emanuel Carlson, executive director of the Baptist Joint Committee on Public Affairs; Mr. John Cogley of the Center for the Study of Democratic Institutions; Mr. Wayne H. Cowan, managing editor of *Christianity and Crisis*; Rev. Robert F. Drinan, S.J., dean of the Law School, Boston College; Rev. Edward Duff, S.J., of Weston College; Mr. Bruce L. Felknor and the staff of the Fair Campaign Practices Committee; Rabbi Arthur Gilbert of the NCCJ; Mr. Emerson Hynes, legislative assistant to Sen. Eugene McCarthy; Dr. Lewis W. Jones, president of the NCCJ; Mr. Dumont Kenny, vice-president for Program Development, NCCJ; Dr. Martin E. Marty, associate editor of *The Christian Century*; Rev. John Courtney Murray, S.J., of Woodstock College, to whom I am particularly indebted for the Foreword to this book; Dr. Claud D. Nelson of the NCCJ; Mrs. Elizabeth Norris, NCCJ librarian; Mother Mary O'Callaghan, associate professor of history, Maryville College; Mr. Philip Scharper of Sheed & Ward, Inc.; Mr. Myron Schwartz of the Jewish Community Relations Council, St. Louis; Dr. Paul G. Steinbicker, director of the Department of Political Science, St. Louis University; Dr. O. Walter Wagner, executive director,

Metropolitan Church Federation of Greater St. Louis; and Mr. Charles C. Webber, AFL-CIO representative for Religious Relations.

I am grateful to the Rockefeller Foundation for the grant which enabled me to carry out the research for this project, and to the editors of *Social Order* for permission to use the article in the June, 1962, issue, "Religion and the 1960 Presidential Election," which constituted a summary version of this book.

CHAPTER ONE

Religion and the Campaign

PRELIMINARY to a content analysis of campaign material,[1] it is necessary, first, to trace the chronology of events related to the religious issue from preconvention days to November 8, 1960; second, to consider the moments of crisis in the fast-moving drama for the insights they provide about the mental and moral fiber of adult America; third, to sort out the individuals and groups directly involved in the public discussion of the religious question and indicate as far as possible their credal alignment and characteristic social and economic orientation; and fourth, to draw some conclusions about the state of the "oldest American prejudice"[2] and its implications for the future of democracy.

PRECONVENTION AND CONVENTION ACTIVITY

Preconvention political activity demonstrated again and again that the religious question was inseparable from the 1960 presidential election. It existed because one of the most prom-

---

[1] Material was obtained from the Fair Campaign Practices Committee; the library of the National Conference of Christians and Jews, New York; the Anti-Defamation League; the files of the Democratic National Committee; and personal interviews and correspondence.

[2] La Salle Woelfel, C.S.C., "The Oldest American Prejudice," *America*, September 24, 1960, pp. 697–699.

inent contenders for the Democratic candidacy was a Catholic. As time went on, the pressure of national reporting focused on the "religious imponderable as the central political question of the campaign."[3] The attempt to win the vice-presidential nomination for Senator Kennedy in 1956 failed, but the circulation of the intriguing Bailey Memorandum among delegates to the Democratic National Convention sparked a lively and prolonged discussion of the "Catholic vote." Looking back to 1952, the Memorandum ascribed the Democratic defeat of that year to the loss of Catholic voters except where a Catholic was on the ticket. In support of the case for Senator Kennedy in 1956, it suggested that a Catholic vice-presidential candidate might refashion the political base among Catholics previously held by the Democratic party.

> If he brought into the Democratic fold only those normally Democratic Catholics who voted for Ike, he would probably swing New York, Massachusetts, Rhode Island, Connecticut, Pennsylvania and Illinois—for 132 electoral votes. If he also wins the votes of Catholics who shifted to the Republicans in 1948 or earlier, he could also swing New Jersey, Minnesota, Michigan, California, Wisconsin, Ohio, Maryland, Montana, and maybe even New Hampshire—for a total of 265 electoral votes (needed to win: 266). Thus Ike could and would be defeated.[4]

In 1958, Kennedy's position as a potential nominee was strengthened by the extraordinary margin of his senatorial re-election victory. Sensitive to this awesome prospect, veteran anti-Catholic forces of bigotry and fear began to mobilize

[3] Theodore H. White, *The Making of the President, 1960,* New York, Atheneum, 1961, p. 92.
[4] "The 'Catholic Vote'—A Kennedy Staff Analysis," *U.S. News and World Report,* August 1, 1960, p. 72.

early in 1959. Senator Kennedy's decision to submit to a kind of religious cross-examination put him on record in favor of religious liberty as envisioned in the American system of separation of church and state, and opposed to public aid for parochial schools and to an ambassador at the Vatican.[5] There followed a flurry of press comment and criticism which coalesced to mark this first peaking of religion as the most discussed topic of the coming campaign. Some commentators thought Mr. Kennedy had gone too far in asserting the primacy of political over other loyalties and had thus deepened the cleavage between religion and public life. For example, *America* editorially registered "impatience at the earnest Massachusetts Senator's efforts to appease bigots" rather than "disagreement with the positive points he made."[6] Dr. Robert McAfee Brown, a friendly Protestant critic, found that in his "effort to assure his possible constituency that he is just a regular American, he has succeeded only in demonstrating that he is a rather irregular Christian."[7] Dr. Martin E. Marty, associate editor of *The Christian Century,* judged that in the instance of Mr.

[5] Fletcher Knebel, "Democratic Forecast: A Catholic in 1960," *Look,* March 3, 1959, pp. 13–17.

[6] In full: "Our own reaction to the controverted *Look* interview is one of impatience at the earnest Massachusetts Senator's efforts to appease bigots, rather than of disagreement with the positive points he made. A Catholic political candidate, if he must make a profession of his faith, should not seem to give quarter to religious bigotry, even at the risk of having his words distorted. We were somewhat taken aback, for instance, by the unvarnished statement that 'whatever one's religion in his private life . . . nothing takes precedence over his oath . . . .' Mr. Kennedy doesn't really believe that. No religious man, be he Catholic, Protestant or Jew, holds such an opinion" ("On Questioning Catholic Candidates," *America,* March 7, 1959, p. 651).

[7] Robert McAfee Brown, "Senator Kennedy's Statement," *Christianity and Crisis,* March 16, 1959, p. 25.

Kennedy "we have a faithful Roman Catholic layman, regular at his worship, but one who is in many ways a son of his time: spiritually rootless and politically almost disturbingly secular."[8]

The affirmation which occasioned these rebukes was the following: "Whatever one's religion in his private life may be, for the officeholder, nothing takes precedence over his oath to uphold the Constitution and all its parts—including the First Amendment and the strict separation of church and state."[9]

On the other hand, there were those who admired the independence and precision with which he crystallized his own conviction about the proper manner in which an elected official should make political decisions. The tone and scope of public reaction in this instance set a pattern which was subsequently repeated with predictable regularity throughout the campaign. Those who admitted a distinction between the man and the "system" declared themselves satisfied with the announced positions of the Democratic aspirant. Some, however, had reservations about his ability to resist the dreaded Vatican and hierarchical pressure.[10] Others could not reconcile his views on religious liberty with the reputed intransigence of Roman Catholicism.

Expressions of doubt, fear, and anxiety about a Catholic

[8] Quoted in "Politics to Decide Election, Protestant Editor Says," *Religious News Service*, October 27, 1960; from an analysis of the religious issues of the campaign for readers of the Dutch newspaper *Het Vrije Volk*.

[9] Knebel, *op. cit.*, p. 17.

[10] "Religion and the Presidency," *Interreligious Newsletter* (published jointly by the American Jewish Commitee and the Anti-Defamation League), October, 1960, p. 6.

presidential candidate grew in number and sharpness during 1959 and the early months of 1960.[11] They came predominantly from Protestant ministers and/or organizations rather than from politicians, although the latter were not averse to using the material when it suited an immediate purpose.[12]

A second peaking of the religious issue occurred at the time of the Wisconsin and West Virginia primaries in April and May of 1960. Analysis of Kennedy's 56-percent Wisconsin majority indicated that he had "lost all four predominantly Protestant districts and had carried the unclassified one (the Seventh) only by a hair. His popular margin had come entirely from four heavily Catholic areas—the Sixth, Eighth, Fourth and Fifth."[13] Thus, the notion that the "Catholic vote" was a pollsters' myth suffered a setback.[14] Paradoxically, the Wiscon-

[11] For an excellent chronology of developments, see *Facts*, June-July, 1960, pp. 158–160; *Facts*, March, 1961, pp. 196–200.

[12] For example, *Religious News Service* reported such typical instances as the following: "Texas Baptists adopted a resolution here cautioning members of the denomination against voting for a Roman Catholic candidate, but noting that 'no person's religious affiliation per se should rule out his candidacy'" (November 6, 1959, p. 7); "Southern Baptists in Oklahoma opposed here [Tulsa] the election of any state or federal candidate who fails to take a 'bold stand' on the Church-State separation principle" (November 16, 1959), p. 14); "Messengers [delegates] to the annual meeting of the Alabama Baptist State Convention here [Montgomery] went on record as protesting against the election of any Roman Catholic as U.S. President" (November 18, 1959, p. 15).

[13] White, *op. cit.*, p. 95.

[14] Elmo Roper, "The Myth of the Catholic Vote," *Saturday Review*, October 31, 1959, p. 22. This article claimed that the 1956 voting statistics showed the "myth" of a precommitted Catholic vote. This opinion was later revised: "But this spring's primaries suggested that with the Presidency at stake, religion had become a matter of much greater importance; and recent survey results confirm its importance for Catholics and non-Catholics alike" (Elmo Roper, "The Catholic Vote: A Second Look," *Saturday Review*, November 5, 1960, p. 27).

sin victory made it imperative for Kennedy to enter and win the other primaries, especially in redoubtable West Virginia. He had to demonstrate in advance to the tough-minded leaders of the coming Democratic Convention his ability to beat the "Catholic question" in states where he was not well known. In West Virginia, religion was pivotal, and the situation was deftly handled by the Kennedy strategists with the spotlight centered on the issue of tolerance. In an area with a 90 to 95 percent Protestant population, Kennedy was the only one who had anything to gain by the West Virginians' exercise of this heralded American virtue. The success of the appeal showed in the May 10 balloting, which gave the Massachusetts Senator such a substantial vote margin that not a few momentarily succumbed to the illusion that the religious handicap had been unduly magnified. That this was not the case became incontestably clear a few months later.

In Washington, D.C., on April 21, 1960, Kennedy addressed the American Society of Newspaper Editors on the subject, "The Religious Issue in American Politics." He refuted point by point the objections to a Catholic President, deplored the tendency of the press to inflate the issue out of all proportion to its importance on the national scene, and challenged his audience to assume greater responsibility in future reporting. Rejecting the suggestion that he withdraw from the presidential contest in order to avoid a nasty religious controversy, he asserted his determination to proceed with the primaries, the Convention, and the election: "If there is bigotry in the country, then so be it—there is bigotry. If that bigotry is too great to permit the fair consideration of a Catholic who has made clear his complete independence and his complete dedication to separation of church and state, then we ought to know it."[15]

Deftly sketched out in this same talk were the ground markers for his campaign appeal to the voters. Premised on the basic unity of the American consensus, the stress fell on the *shared* experience of *all* citizens in allegiance to the Constitution, with a liberality of mind and heart and an openness to the future. The refrain of "belonging" was the key in which the comprehensive, coordinated, and ultimately victorious strategy was pitched. Americans were summoned, in the name of what they all held sacred, to meet the domestic and international challenges of the troubled present and the uncertain future.

After Senator Kennedy won the Democratic nomination at the July Convention, the religious issue became less speculative and more concrete, less rational and more emotional. In accepting the candidacy, he made clear his hope that

. . . no American, considering the really critical issues facing this country, will waste his franchise by voting either for me or against me solely on account of my religious affiliation. It is not relevant, I want to stress, whatever some other political or religious leader may have said on this subject. It is not relevant what abuses may have existed in other countries or in other times. It is not relevant what pressures, if any, might conceivably be brought to bear on me. I am telling you now what you are entitled to know: that my decisions on every public policy will be my own—as an American, a Democrat and a free man.[16]

[15] John F. Kennedy, "Text of Address to American Society of Newspaper Editors," Washington, D.C., April 21, 1960, *U.S. News and World Report*, May 2, 1960, pp. 90–92.

[16] Senator John F. Kennedy, speech of acceptance as presidential nominee to the Democratic National Convention, July 15, 1960, as printed in *U.S. News and World Report*, July 25, 1960, p. 100.

THE GATHERING MOMENTUM

Nevertheless, religion again peaked as the top campaign topic early in September with the Washington meeting of the National Conference of Citizens for Religious Freedom. A barrage of unwanted publicity was turned on this *ad hoc* anti-Catholic group of 150 Protestants led by such notables as Dr. Norman Vincent Peale; Dr. Daniel A. Poling, editor of the *Christian Herald;* Dr. L. M. Bell, an editor of *Christianity Today;* Dr. Glenn Archer, executive director of Protestants and Other Americans United for Separation of Church and State (POAU); Rev. Donald Gill of the National Association of Evangelicals; J. Elwin Wright, and Dr. Harold J. Ockenga.[17] The day-long gathering concluded with a statement embodying five points of criticism against the Catholic Church, charging that it is a "political as well as a religious organization"; has "specifically repudiated on many occasions the principle sacred to us that every man shall be free to follow the dictates of his conscience in religious matters"; has a record in other countries of "denial of equal rights for all other faiths"; has repeatedly tried to "break down the wall of separation of church and state by a continuous campaign to secure public funds for the support of its schools and other institutions"; and would not permit a President of this faith "to participate in interfaith meetings."[18]

[17] Douglas Cater, "The Protestant Issue," *Reporter,* October 13, 1960, pp. 30–32.

[18] Text in Appendix B. The Citizens for Religious Freedom carried on the battle against the Catholic candidate through *News and Notes* brochures and the strenuous efforts of individuals. Prominent among the latter was Lt. Gen. W. K. Harrison, U.S. Army (ret.).

On the same day, POAU issued a statement in its own name which said in part:

> Nevertheless, we cannot avoid recognition of the fact that one church in the U.S., the largest church operating on American soil, officially supports a world-wide policy of partial union of church and state wherever it has the power to enforce such a policy. In the U.S. the bishops of this church have specifically rejected the Supreme Court's interpretation of the separation of church and state.[19]

Leading Protestants promptly protested, with the most effective response coming in a joint statement by Dr. Reinhold Niebuhr, former vice-president of Union Theological Seminary, and Dr. John Bennett, dean of the faculty at Union. These two eminent theologians accused the Peale group and its POAU partner of loosing the "floodgates of bigotry clothed in the respectability of apparently rational argument,"[20] and said that the shallowness of the argument was evidenced by its failure to grasp the comprehensiveness of Catholicism and its tendency to concentrate exclusively on allegedly undesirable features, especially those of the past; the "inner dynamics of Roman Catholicism" were ignored along with the "freedom of the Catholic layman in civil affairs." The appalling blindness to the diversity of opinion, policy, and practice among Catholics from country to country, they held, was matched by the deplorable implication that no Roman Catholic should ever be President, no matter what his views on the essential issues.

In a searing judgment, a writer in *The Christian Century* saw the episode as a betrayal of the finest in the Protestant

[19] U.S. *News and World Report,* September 19, 1960, p. 97.
[20] "Text of Statement on Religious Issue," *New York Times,* September 16, 1960, p. 18.

15

tradition of respect for individual freedom and personal belief —a misrepresentation of "the breadth of Protestant interests, the intelligence of Protestant concerns, the charity of Protestant attitudes."[21]

A number of other Protestant leaders broke sharply with the anti-Catholic surge. In Dallas, after the stinging July 3 sermon of Rev. W. A. Criswell at the First Baptist Church, Rev. Baxton Bryant, a Methodist pastor, demanded equal time for a radio broadcast entitled "A Plea for American Fair Play." Reverend Criswell charged that the election of Kennedy would "spell the death of a free church in a free state . . . and our hopes of continuance of full religious liberty in America."[22] Reverend Bryant replied that "America cannot afford in this time of crisis to write off forty million of its citizens as unfit for leadership on account of religious prejudice."[23] The result was a heavy influx of mail almost evenly split between applause and abuse.[24]

Among the major Protestant publications which objected to raising the religious issue in the campaign were *World Outlook*, the organ of the Board of Missions of the Methodist Church; *The Crusader* (September 12, 1960 issue); the official publication of the American Baptist Convention; and *Christianity and Crisis*, an interdenominational journal of opinion.

A persistent thread in the fabric of opposition to Mr. Ken-

---

[21] "Religious Smoke Screen," *Christian Century*, September 21, 1960, p. 1076.

[22] Michael Daves, "Religious Fracas in Dallus," *Christian Century*, October 12, 1960, p. 1181.

[23] *Ibid.*

[24] Philip Geylin, "The Religious Issue," *Wall Street Journal*, September 12, 1960, p. 14.

nedy stemmed from economic conservatives, Catholic and Protestant alike. Their willingness to use religion as a shield against an economic policy which might be expected under a liberal Democratic President belied the profundity of their vaunted commitment to freedom of worship. According to Rev. Jess Moody, a Southern Baptist minister of Owensboro, Kentucky, anti-Catholic literature sent out from some Protestant sources was financed by "businessmen opposed to Kennedy because of his liberal economic policies rather than his religion."[25] Another observer, speaking of the flood of hate-and-fear leaflets sent across the land, commented:

> The clergy who lent their names to this assault are often not merely anti-Catholic but also the same who have peddled the line that the more liberal Protestant clergy affiliated with the respected National Council of Churches of Christ are rotten-infiltrated with Communists. Almost certainly most of the campaign was bankrolled by conservative businessmen of the type who in other elections have financed slanderous pamphlets on union officials; businessmen whose real fear is not of Kennedy's religious faith but of Kennedy as a liberal Democrat running on a liberal platform.[26]

CLARIFICATIONS AND COMPLICATIONS OF THE ISSUE

A significant landmark, the fruit of noteworthy advances in intergroup dialogue, was the "Statement on Religious Liberty in Relation to the 1960 National Campaign" which appeared

[25] "Religious Issue Just Reactionary Excuse," *Labor World,* October 6, 1960. The same point was made in James Reston, "Dallas: Economic and Religious Coalition in Texas," *New York Times,* September 14, 1960.
[26] Willard Shelton, "The Presidency," *American Federationist,* October, 1960, p. 7.

on September 12, 1960. Signed by 100 distinguished Americans of the Catholic, Protestant, Greek Orthodox, and Jewish faiths, it had been initiated and carefully prepared by wise and courageous Protestant leaders who were eager for more than a purely defensive posture. The focal point of their common concern was aptly spelled out:

> The judgment of God finds us at a particular moment in history, confronted by its unique challenges and dilemmas, and it is there that our testing is. In the circumstances that now confront us, we must act according to our principles, or be found wanting. In the election campaign of 1960 we face a real and inescapable challenge with respect to the relation between a man's religion and the responsibility of the nation's highest elective office.

The signers agreed that the "religious faith of a public officer is relevant to the conduct of his office," but that in a pluralistic society he must also recognize "the values in historic faiths other than his own," and bring them "to bear upon the problems of the day." The first of the ten guidelines proposed for voters in the 1960 election stated flatly: "The exclusion of members of any family of faith from public office on the basis of religious affiliation violates the fundamental conditions of a free democratic society, as expressed in the spirit of our Constitution."[27] Hailed as "the most important doctrinal statement on religious liberty, made during these last few months,"[28] the document showed a fine sense of fellowship, a keen awareness of healthy diversity within Roman Catholicism, and an intelligent concern for a proper pluralism.

[27] Text in Appendix B.
[28] A. F. Carrillo De Albornoz, "Ecumenical Chronicle: Religious Liberty from Day to Day," *Ecumenical Review*, July, 1961, p. 477.

September 12, 1960, was also the date of the heralded address by Senator Kennedy before the Greater Houston Ministerial Association. A number of factors prompted the bold decision to face the religious issue squarely at this particular moment and in a militantly Protestant setting. Intelligence data across the country agreed that Catholicism was inextricably involved in the campaign, and that the best way to handle the problem was to meet the accusers, the skeptical, and the uncommitted in direct personal confrontation. One of the most fascinating reports was delivered to Democratic Manager Robert Kennedy on August 25 by the Simulmatics Corporation.[29] Estimating future voter reaction to the religious issue according to a mathematical model processed by an IBM 704 computor, the simulation section of the report indicated that Kennedy had already lost all the votes he would lose as a result of anti-Catholicism. It suggested, moreover, that exacerbation of the religious issue might work to his advantage, and, at any rate, "he would not lose further from forthright and persistent attention to the religious issue, and could gain."[30]

The speech followed a concise, concatinated classical pattern, with a careful balancing of dichotomous couplets. The attention of the audience was directed to the kind of America the nominee envisioned.

I believe in an America where the separation of church and state is absolute—where no Catholic prelate would tell the President (should he be Catholic) how to act, and no Protestant minister would tell his parishioners for whom to vote—where no church or church school is

[29] Thomas B. Morgan, "The People-Machine," *Harper's*, January, 1961, pp. 53–57.
[30] *Ibid.*, p. 54.

19

granted any public funds or political preference—and where no man is denied public office merely because his religion differs from the President who might appoint him or the people who might elect him.

I believe in an America that is officially neither Catholic, Protestant nor Jewish—where no public official either requests or accepts instructions on public policy from the Pope, the National Council of Churches or any other ecclesiastical source—where no religious body seeks to impose its will directly or indirectly upon the general populace or the public acts of its officials—and where religious liberty is so indivisible that an act against one church is treated as an act against all.

On the profoundly relevant point of the relation of the President's conscience to his public decisions, Mr. Kennedy was clear: "Whatever issue may come before me as President—on birth control, divorce, censorship, gambling, or any other subject—I will make my decision in accordance with these views, in accordance with what my conscience tells me to be the national interest, and without regard to outside religious pressures or dictates."[31]

The American public had apparently not yet grasped the central distinction between *what* a man conscientiously stands for in policy matters and *how* his conscience is formed. People may legitimately inquire about the former, but not about the latter; the constitutional protection of religious liberty prohibits a prescribed manner of forming consciences. To think otherwise would be to totalitarianize democracy. One of the most harped-on charges, nevertheless, was that a Catholic Chief Executive would be the target of omnipresent ecclesiastical pressures seeking to influence his deliberations.

The Houston speech succeeded in allaying fears and dispell-

[31] Text in Appendix B.

ing doubts, and it appears in retrospect as a turning point in the uphill campaign. A typical audience reaction came from Rev. John W. Turnbull, associate professor of Christian ethics at the Episcopal Seminary of the Southwest in Austin, Texas, who thought that the young Catholic Senator did very well in an "inquisition-like" atmosphere. "Whose loyalty to the Constitution which separates church and state and forbids religious tests for public office was really open to question? His or our?"[32]

In addition to those from avowed conservatives preoccupied with economic considerations, attacks on Senator Kennedy because of his religion came from several identifiable types. The most vicious, though the least effective politically, were the professional peddlers of hate literature—the "apostles of discord."[33] Prominent in this category were Brig. Gen. Herbert C. Holdridge (ret.) of Sherman Oaks, California, who viewed all things in terms of the machinations of a "Jesuit-Vatican Axis"; Reverend Carl McIntire of Collingswood, New Jersey, deposed from the ministry of the Presbyterian Church in the U.S.A. and the editor of the weekly *Christian Beacon*; Rev. Harrison Parker, "Chancellor" of a Washington, D.C., Puritan Church; Rev. Bob Shuler of Los Angeles, California, publisher of *The Methodist Challenge*, an anti-Catholic sheet; and Rev. Harvey Springer of Englewood, Colorado, the "cowboy evangelist" and anti-Roman pamphleteer. The National Association

[32] Rev. John W. Turnbull, "The Clergy Faces Mr. Kennedy," *Reporter*, October 13, 1960, pp. 32–34.

[33] Ralph Lord Roy, *Apostles of Discord: A Study of Organized Bigotry and Disruption on the Fringes of Protestantism*, Boston, Beacon, 1953.

of Evangelicals, a fundamentalist organization with about two million members,[34] served as a springboard for the anti-Catholic forces. Teamed up with members of the Southern Baptist Convention and POAU, they turned out millions of pieces of campaign literature to stop Kennedy. During the last two weeks of September and the first two of October, 1960, the NAE sent out a letter under the signature of its president, Thomas F. Zimmerman, to pastors in churches throughout the nation urging the adoption of a "plan of action" to this end. The plan was explained in a form letter, and a kit of material was available on request, including such items as "A Roman Catholic President—How Free From Church Control?" by Dr. George I. Ford, and "Where Does Your Church Stand in Times Like These?" Responses by mid-October had been received from an estimated 6000 to 7000 churches.[35] Most Protestant groups, however, even those with serious hesitations about the Catholic Church, went on record against such anti-Catholic attitudes and urged their members to disregard the religious issue in making their political selection.

A noteworthy development in Catholic lay initiative occurred on October 5 with the publication of "A Statement on Religious Liberty by American Catholic Laymen," signed by 166 recognized leaders in academic and professional fields. Incisive and closely reasoned, the document contained an excellent presen-

[34] Joe Thomas, "How Widespread Is Bias? Election to Give Answer," *Advocate*, November 3, 1960.
[35] Robert S. Bird and Jo-Ann Price, "All-out Religious Attack on Kennedy Planned by 38 Fundamentalist Sects," *New York Herald Tribune*, October 16, 1960, pp. 1, 40.

tation of the view held by most American Catholics, but scarcely known to be so held, about the relationship of religion and the free society. The signatories affirmed their belief in the freedom of religious conscience and the obligation of Catholics in all nations to work for the realization of this principle as a legally recognized and officially protected civil right. The Catholic laymen praised the constitutional separation of church and state, underscored "the freedom of a church to teach its members and the freedom of its members to accept the teachings of their church," denied to civil society the right to inquire "how a citizen forms his conscience," and affirmed the duty of public officials, whatever their religious persuasion, to promote the common good of the whole community and to refrain from seeking purely sectarian advantage.[36] They made their own the words of Cardinal Lercaro, Archbishop of Bologna, Italy, that the Catholic's commitment to religious liberty "is not a concession suggested by prudence and grudgingly made to the spirit of the times," but is rooted in the "permanent principles of Catholicism."[37] Whatever the statement's impact on the many who doubted the firmness of Catholic endorsement of religious freedom, it encouraged the few who were willing to listen and spurred the hopes of all who

[36] Text in Appendix B. The statement was mimeographed and distributed to the press and reprinted in a number of papers.

[37] Giacomo Cardinal Lercaro, "Tolérance et intolérance religieuse," Documentation Catholique, March 15, 1959, pp. 335–347, tr. in Catholic Mind, January-February, 1960. The right to freedom of religious conscience is carefully and cogently argued by Eric D'Arcy: "Two conclusions only have been argued: the obligation to follow one's conscience when it has been formed in good faith; and the right to follow it, with freedom from State interference, in matters of religious faith, profession and worship" (Conscience and Its Right to Freedom, New York, Sheed & Ward, 1961, p. 272).

23

had come to expect much from the burgeoning lay movement in the United States.

The amazing timing of the double thrust into domestic politics by the Puerto Rican prelates, coming as it did in mid-October, lent strong psychological support to the anti-Kennedy forces. The Democratic candidate predictably stood his ground, but the affair seemed to many Americans a glaring application of the controversial article "*Punti Fermi*," which had appeared in the May 18, 1960, issue of *Osservatore Romano*.[38] This editorial was a four-point assertion of the Church's competence in applying moral norms to political and social problems in accordance with Pius IX's *Syllabus*. It was widely known that Cardinal Tardini, then papal secretary of state, was opposed to the restatement at this juncture and was willing to be quoted to that effect. Its impact in the United Sates, however, was irreversible, especially in the light of the subsequent overt opposition by the bishops of Puerto Rico to the Popular Democratic Party of Governor Luis Muñoz Marín.

THE HOME STRETCH

A coalition of conservative Protestant churchmen had conspired to make Reformation Sunday, October 30, 1960, the occasion for launching a gigantic home-stretch drive to defeat Senator Kennedy. But an effective intramural Protestant dialogue succeeded in targeting many of the sermons against bigotry rather than against Catholicism as originally planned. Ministers who mentioned the issue did so only to condemn

38 "*Punti Fermi*," *Osservatore Romano*, May 18, 1960, p. 1.

the use of the pulpit as a political platform and turned their attention to Protestantism's centuries-old traditions. In New York, for example, Dr. Robert J. McCracken, senior minister of Riverside Church, declared that it was "wrong to use Reformation Day to stir up anti-Catholic feeling."[39] Dr. John Heuss, rector of Trinity Episcopal Parish, preaching in St. Paul's Chapel, New York, said that he did not share the view "that Senator Kennedy constitutes a threat to American freedom because of his religion."[40] For the first time in many years no mass Reformation Day rallies were held in St. Louis, Missouri; instead, more than 30 churches observed the anniversary with special services in their own sanctuaries.[41]

In the final tense days of the campaign, everyone knew that religion was a foremost concern of voters, but no one knew how it would influence their choice in the polling booths on November 8. The magnitude and virulence of the anti-Catholic material flooding the country reached unprecedented dimensions during the first week of November. Much of it was professionally printed and distributed in a wide variety of forms— as editorials, sermons, leaflets, reprints of sermons, press releases, church publications, speeches, and pamphlets. Appeals to bigotry were matched by reverse bigotry and the whole compounded by the mushrooming of committees in defense of "liberty" of one kind or another.[42]

The tide of the election returns reported over the national

[39] " 'Religious Issue' Plays Minor Role in Reformation Sermons," *Religious News Service*, October 31, 1960, p. 1.
[40] *Ibid.*, p. 2.
[41] *Ibid.*, p. 3.
[42] "Frenzied Final Week Ended '60 Campaign," *Bulletin of the Fair Campaign Practices Committee*, April, 1961, pp. 2–3.

broadcasting systems the night of November 8–9 rose and fell in strange, unpredictable swells. The outcome, in fact, remained uncertain for many days and weeks, with the final tabulation showing a popular vote of 49.7 percent for the Democratic and 49.6 percent for the Republicans. In 1960, as in 1928, post-election studies disagreed about religion's impact on the close tally. There is fairly general agreement that four out of five Catholics voted for Kennedy, and less than two out of five of the nation's Protestants.[43]

The high estimate (IBM) is that 46 percent of all American Protestants voted for John F. Kennedy, or 22,500,000—making almost two thirds of his total. The low estimate (Dr. George Gallup) is that only 38 per cent of all American Protestants voted for John F. Kennedy—which still comes to some 18,600,000 of his 34,000,000 constituency, or critically more than half of his majority.[44]

PARTISANS OF FREEDOM

Full credit should be given to all who made outstanding contributions to fair play during the campaign. Most Jewish organizations were fearless and forthright in demanding that candidates for public office be judged on their individual merit and not as members of religious, racial, or ethnic groups. The American Jewish Committee concentrated its influential efforts against the "divisive myth of bloc voting,"[45] denying the

[43] Philip E. Converse, "Religion and Politics: The 1960 Elections," paper delivered at the Annual Meeting of the American Sociological Association, St. Louis, August-September, 1961, p. 3.

[44] White, op. cit., p. 357.

[45] "American Jewish Committee Statement on Bloc Voting," News (released by the American Jewish Committee, Institute of Human Relations), September 2, 1960; see also John Slawson, "Guidelines: The Bloc Voting Myth," Committee Reporter, October, 1960, pp. 6–7, 28.

existence of packages of precommitted votes. So, too, the American Jewish Congress labeled the concept "guilt by association" an "anathema to freedom," and warned that "injecting the religious issue into the Presidential election campaign might give rise to the development of religious political parties in the United States."[46]

The Anti-Defamation League of B'nai B'rith performed a valuable service by reporting day-to-day events and collecting and exposing "hate" literature.[47] A resolution adopted by the General Board of the National Council of Churches of Christ in the U.S.A. stressed the responsibility of its members "to vigorously oppose appeals to religious bigotry as a factor in elections. Voting should be based primarily upon a candidate's personal integrity, his leadership competence, and his stand on central issues."[48]

Particularly significant was the splendid work of the National Conference of Christians and Jews and the Fair Campaign Practices Committee in combating religious prejudice during the campaign. NCCJ efforts included an Interreligious Dialogue in Washington, D.C., on March 24–25, 1960, co-sponsored by the FCPC; a series of practical directives from NCCJ President Lewis Webster Jones to regional staffs for guidance in promoting a fair campaign; a one-minute filmed

[46] "Religion and the Presidency," *Interreligious Newsletter,* October, 1960, p. 7.
[47] "The Religious Issue in the Presidential Campaign," *Facts,* June-July, 1960; "The 1960 Election Campaign," *Facts,* March, 1961.
[48] "Christian Responsibility in the 1960 Elections," a resolution adopted by the General Board of the National Council of the Churches of Christ in the U.S.A., New York, NCCC, Office of Publication and Distribution, February 25, 1960.

27

spot announcement for TV use; and a luncheon news conference held jointly with the Morris Morgenstern Foundation to commemorate the hundred and seventieth anniversary of George Washington's famous letter to the Touro Synagogue in Newport, Rhode Island, containing the phrase, "To bigotry no sanction, to persecution no assistance."[49]

The Fair Campaign Practices Committee was established in 1954 in response to congressional and public concern over the excesses of the 1950 and 1952 campaigns. The Committee adopted a Code of Fair Campaign Practices and, in cooperation with the Democratic and Republican National Committees, asked all congressional candidates to give public assurance of abiding by the Code.[50] In 1960, some 80 percent of the candidates for gubernatorial and congressional offices signed the Code, as compared with 85 percent in 1958 and 70 percent in 1956.[51] The Committee continues to perform a multiple service of public education by promoting the Code signing, providing information on techniques used in unfair practices, handling complaints and serving as a clearing house for campaign literature and other valuable political artifacts. State-by-state smear studies undertaken by the FCPC after the 1956 and 1958 elections indicated with amazing accuracy the shape of things to come in 1960. The 1958 report, for example, showed that there had been a decrease of anti-Semitism and a sharp increase of anti-Catholicism.[52] The 1960 study, released in

[49] *Religious News Service*, October 26, 1960, p. 12.
[50] *Fair Play in Politics* (pamphlet), New York, Fair Campaign Practices Committee, 1960, p. 7.
[51] "Code Signed in 80 Per Cent of Races," *Bulletin of the Fair Campaign Practices Committee*, April, 1961, p. 4.
[52] *Fair Play in Politics*, p. 12.

February, 1962, contains an excellent summary and analysis of 1383 reports of 402 unfair anti-Catholic political attacks and some 392 pieces of unfair anti-Catholic political literature.

The states in which these tracts originated fall into a curious pattern. Despite predictable pressure from the "Bible belt," three states outside of this zone were the source of one-third of the total volume: California (60 pieces), Pennsylvania (41), and Minnesota (35). Although the volume of printed matter dealing with the religious issue in the 1960 campaign was substantially greater than in 1928, the quality was, on the whole, higher. "If the number of tracts in 1960 addressing the question of a Catholic in the White House were apportioned among four categories, in descending order of offensiveness, the tally would show something like this: Vile   5%; Dishonest 25%; Unfair 35%; Responsible 35%."[53] FCPC Executive Director Bruce L. Felknor observed perceptively in 1959:

Religion, because of its capacity to rouse emotions and to generate zeal, can be a most dangerous ingredient in elections. Our faiths differ, but they focus on one God, a God of love and a God of vengeance. Perhaps our chore is to seek, in this borderland between the exaltation of God and the election of government, ways to temper our human reactions with His love, and to leave vengeance to Him."[54]

CONCLUSION

This is the record of the campaign. What conclusion can be drawn about the "oldest American prejudice"? Very little from

[53] The State-by-State Study of Smear: 1960," *Report of the Fair Campaign Practices Committee,* February, 1962, p. 16.
[54] Bruce L. Felknor, "Bigotry in Forthcoming Election Campaigns," address to the National Conference of Christians and Jews, Commission on Religious Organizations, Committee on Religious Liberty, April 15, 1959.

the mere chronology of events and very much from a probing examination of the substantive content of the literature mentioned above. Only the natively naive would write it off as a dead relic of the pioneer past or a marginal note of the more sophisticated present; ample evidence shows the issue to be alive and active in the masses of the American electorate. In one sense, nothing essential seems to have been altered since 1928, but in another, emerging patterns of psychological and social adjustment suggest a future of more profound and fruitful interfaith advances. The United States has passed a milestone on the road of religious pluralism. Roman Catholicism has gained a modicum of social acceptance, and responsible Protestantism and Judaism have effectively demonstrated the practical meaning of individual liberty and fair play.

CHAPTER TWO

The Substantive Issues:
Catholicism and American Democracy

ACCORDING to the Fair Campaign Practices Committee, some 392 different anti-Catholic pieces of all kinds were circulated during the campaign with an estimated total circulation of between 20,000,000 and 25,000,000. This literature presents an undeclinable invitation to trace the trite theme of continuity and change in the history of American religious tensions. The optimist will be grateful for the progress which is indicated, and the realist appalled at the rhythmic regularity of repetition. A mosaic of paradoxes emerges from the assembled strands which in some fashion reflect the texture of contemporary American thinking on church-state problems. Prominent among the paradoxes posed by the ensemble are the following:

1. A decades-long recession of religious influence on the culture and public institutions of the nation was suddenly reversed by a revival of religious battles, not over internal matters of doctrine and worship but for political control of the country.

2. The widespread Protestant fear of Roman Catholic suppression of religious liberty was deliberately subordinated to the constitutional proscription of a religious test for public office by those courageous sons of the Reformation who remained loyal to their tradition of respect for religious freedom.

3. A progressive presidential candidate professing an allegedly conservative and reactionary Catholicism, was defended by liberal Protestants and by certain writers in secular journals against attacks by a coalition of fundamentalists and rationalist freethinkers.

4. The American system of separation of church and state, accepted by all religious groups, is considered by Catholics to be rooted in *politics,* and by the heirs of the free-church tradition to be rooted in *religion.* The Baptists, in particular, find its source in the theological concept of the free human being's relationship with his God. Catholics see in the First Amendment a legal/constitutional arrangement of the natural order, which is subject to its own civil laws and distinct from the supernatural order of grace and faith.

5. A country which prides itself on a nondoctrinal, pragmatic approach to politics became embroiled in a bitter religious controversy over the "official" Catholic *doctrine* on Church-state relations.

6. A nation with proven prowess in technological and industrial fields and a high level of literacy among its population footnoted its objections to a Catholic President with ancient documents and dated artifacts, while showing scant familiarity with modern Catholic writing on church-state matters.

7. The loudest clamor against a Catholic President came not from residents of crowded urban centers who had long rubbed elbows with Catholic neighbors and presumably suffered civic disabilities from encounters with Catholic political power, but from natives of rural areas where Catholics scarcely abound.

So much for the paradoxes. But what of the argument?

32

THE ESSENCE OF THE ANTI-CATHOLIC ARGUMENT

Insofar as it can be rationally formulated from campaign literature, the pivotal charge against Catholicism centers in the supposed threat to American freedom posed by an inflexible religio-political system, authoritarian and monolithic in structure and rigidly controlled from Rome, bent on dominating the United States and eventually the whole world. Subsumed under this comprehensive indictment are a number of particular items which regularly recur in the source material:

1. Roman Catholicism does not accept, on principle, the American system of separation of church and state as embodied in the First Amendment, but abides by it as a matter of expediency. The threat to the liberties of non-Catholics is consequently proportionate to the political power which Catholics achieve, since they are conscience-bound to implement the "established church" doctrine whenever this becomes possible.

2. Catholics have a "dual allegiance," to the Pope in Rome and to the United States, with priority automatically accorded to the former in cases of conflict.

3. The "hierarchy" controls the decisions of Catholic laymen in all matters, even those that are strictly political.

4. The immediate aim of the Church in this country is to procure public money for its schools and to enact Catholic morality into civil law on such issues as birth control, marriage, and medical practices.

5. Wealth and moral laxity too often characterize the lives of the Catholic clergy.

33

It is obviously beyond the scope of this study to attempt an adequate presentation of the credentials of Roman Catholicism; complete explanation of so complex a phenomenon eludes capture by the written word, which would crystallize it on the printed page and ignore the inherent dynamic of its development and the unfathomable mystery of its inner being. It is precisely the willingness to settle for a superficial knowledge drawn from scanning official and unofficial documents which accounts for many faulty notions about the origin, nature, and purposes of the Catholic Church. Those who aspire to some measure of accurate understanding must be prepared to seek it in the centuries-old history of the Church, its emergence from Old Testament promises, its establishment by Christ—as a juridical structure as well as a divine-human community, and its continued existence in time, carrying on the threefold ministry of teaching, governing, and sanctifying men. There is a need for familiarity, too, with the key concept of the development of doctrine, which provides insights into the distinction between permanent principles and the contingent modes of their manifestation. The late Pius XII deplored the error that would conceive of the Church as "petrified at some historical moment and debarred from any further development."[1] On the contrary, he pointed to "the need and significance of her vital law of continuous adaptation, which some, incapable of grasping such a magnificent concept, have interpreted or described as opportunism."[2]

Catholicism's claim to be the one true religion founded by

[1] Pius XII, "The Church—Foundation of Society," *Catholic Mind*, April, 1946, p. 197.
[2] *Ibid.*, p. 198.

34

Christ raises the practical problem of the proper stance for such a Church vis à vis the manifold temporal institutions of society. The relationship between church and state is but one aspect of this larger topic. The whole question must of necessity be considered in historical perspective because the concrete issues at stake in a given situation arise in widely different social and political contexts and call for appropriate contingent arrangements. The only permanent principles which the Church has always insisted upon are (1) the distinct origin, function, and power of the two societies—church and state, (2) the primacy of the spiritual power, (3) freedom of the Church, and (4) some mode of harmonious collaboration between the two powers. All else is relative to time, place, and the level of political maturity of the local citizenry. The contemporary Church is concerned with preserving the spiritual character of her authority while acknowledging the legitimate autonomy of the temporal order. Her influence on the institutions of society is indirect, that is, channeled through the individual man who is at once Christian and citizen. A democracy respects the freedom of each man to respond to the teachings of his church and at the same time to participate in the political processes of the nation.

UNION OF CHURCH AND STATE IN CATHOLIC THOUGHT

The paramount anxiety about the Church, registered in campaign literature at all levels of sophistication, was the notion that Catholics are inevitably committed to the union of church and state as an absolute ideal. Hence the feeling that the American Catholic's professed allegiance to the First Amendment is, at best, a matter of expediency to be jettisoned when a favorable balance of power permits, and, at worst, an aspect of the Vatican plot to simulate tolerance and thus dull the vigilance of naive non-Catholics. Cited in support of the argument are statements of approved writers and incidents of recorded history, ancient and modern. Predictably popular among the latter are happenings in Spain, Portugal, and Colombia, and among the former the works of Gregory XVI, Leo XIII, Pius IX (especially the *Syllabus*), the articles of A. Messineo, S.J., in *La Civiltà Cattolica*, and *Catholic Principles of Politics* by Ryan and Boland. Almost unmentioned are the works of those Catholics who defend religious liberty in principle as perfectly compatible with Catholic teaching. Proponents of this latter view are unhappy with the thesis-hypothesis dichotomy and do not consider that a constitutionally established church is an irreversible Catholic doctrine or even an essential consequence thereof.[3] They assert that a coherent theory must be mindful of legal and political as well as theological realities. Thus, while religious unity among men is the will of God, absolutely speaking, religious division is the existential human condition. These Catholics insist that the distinction between the two authorities by which the life of man is ruled—church and state—involves the further distinction, first, between the order of divine law and the order of human

[3] The best account of this view is contained in A. F. Carrillo De Albornoz, *Roman Catholicism and Religious Liberty*, Geneva, World Council of Churches, 1959. More recent developments are treated in various articles of a "Symposium on Religious Liberty," *Ecumenical Review*, July, 1961

law, and second, between the attitude of the Church toward what is true and right and the attitude of the state toward what is politically prudent and conducive to the common good. The norm for the statesman's decision-making is that of the temporal common good in a given set of circumstances. Suppression of evil is not per se good, nor the toleration of evil per se evil.

In the light of the intramural division among Catholic thinkers, how valid is the standard Protestant assertion that official Catholic doctrine is expressed in the established-church thesis? How well-founded is the fear, so evident during the campaign, that Catholics, once in a dominant position, might feel bound to rescind the First Amendment guarantees of religious freedom? Are Protestants and others justified in asking that the separation of church and state be given authoritative endorsement at the ecclesiastical summit?[4]

These questions do not readily yield to simple, single, categorical answers, nor are they to be brushed aside as irrelevant. Regarding doctrine, the established-church thesis does not have infallible status, and probably the best it can claim is a "traditional main-line position."[5] The Church has not fully and finally fashioned her attitude on religious liberty as it is understood in modern pluralist democracies like the United States. Experience, however, suggests that freedom from favor

[4] This urgent and sincere plea was appositely stated by Rev. John Sutherland Bonnell: "There is such a fog of confusion and uncertainty enveloping this entire subject in Roman Catholic teaching that the Catholic Church would render a service to the whole Christian world, and to itself in particular, if it would make an unequivocal pronouncement on church-state relations" ("Religion and the Presidency," *Presbyterian Life*, May 1, 1960, p. 10).

[5] John C. Bennett, *Christians and the State*, New York, Scribner's, 1958, p. 264.

can indeed be more desirable than privilege and protection. Mounting, too, are the problems of the tangled pluralism of Asia, Africa, and the Middle East where Catholic must compete with Hindu, Muslim, Buddhist, and Shintoist as well as with Protestant, Greek Orthodox, Jew, and secular humanist.

The ambiguity of the present situation was recently summed up in two estimates which ended in the same unanswered query: has the Church in the course of some decades changed its stand on the question of religious freedom? From the Catholic side, the editor of *Perspectives* noted that the fundamental concept of the *magisterium* underlies the campaign issues about the degree of Catholic commitment to the ideal of the confessional state and the extent of hierarchical control over the layman as citizen and public official:

In the present situation the interesting point is whether or not the liberal sentiments and attitudes expressed by Catholics and seemingly sanctioned by proper authority do not seem to demand certain modifications in the very concept of the magisterial power of the Church. The alternative to such a searching inquiry would be the depressing admission that during the campaign a seriously misleading impression was allowed to gain currency and that we did not have quite enough courage to spell out the true picture.[6]

Likewise, from the Protestant side comes this opinion:

With regard to *Roman Catholic doctrine* on religious freedom, we must register a peculiar situation. The partisans of intolerance are still numerous, but silent. Since the temperamental outburst of Cardinal Ottaviani in 1953, no single authoritative voice of the Vatican has been raised against religious liberty. On the contrary, authoritative statements in favor of freedom of religion have frequently occurred so that the

[6] James J. Maguire, editorial, *Perspectives*, January-February, 1961, p. 3.

recently published booklet on "Roman Catholicism and Religious Liberty" is no longer up to date.[7]

Such well-known American Catholics as Rev. John Courtney Murray, S.J., Rev. Gustave Weigel, S.J., and Rev. John A. O'Brien are not alone on the list of those favoring the "liberal" view. Included also are Cardinal Döpfner, Bishop of Berlin, Cardinal Montini, Archbishop of Milan, and Dr. Gerhard Kroll, the prominent German politician. Noteworthy, too, was a Pax Romana resolution of January, 1961, affirming that the "right of every man to religious liberty, should be recognized and guaranteed by the state."[8]

The contemporary orientation of an ever-widening spectrum of Catholic thought was further evidenced in a pastoral letter issued by the hierarchy of Tanganyika in 1961. Denying any right of the state over the religious convictions of its citizens, the letter affirms the duty of civil society to protect freedom of religion, which implies

. . . first, that the State cannot force any citizen to practice a religion and perform the acts of a cult repugnant to his conscience; secondly, in acquitting itself of its responsibilities toward the public, the State must do so in the best interests of all and with complete impartiality as regards beliefs and religions; finally, that no public servant have any right to show himself biased in favour of his coreligionists in the carrying out of his duties, still less is he entitled to take advantage of his position as a servant of the public to favour unduly the organs of any particular religious persuasion.[9]

[7] A. F. Carrillo De Albornoz, "Ecumenical Chronicle: Religious Liberty from Day to Day," *Ecumenical Review,* July, 1961, p. 479
[8] *Ibid.,* p. 481.
[9] "The Church in a Plural Society: Portions from a Pastoral Letter Issued by Cardinal Rugambwa and the Archbishops and Bishops of Tanganyika," *Christian Democrat,* May, 1961, pp. 226–227.

What should be the attitude of the lay Catholic living in a pluralistic society? The Tanganyikan bishops are incisive:

> The illusion of comfort and security of a "Ghetto-centered" existence is a sorry type of peace and not the dynamic love of Neighbour which should take us to every place where we can serve. Only by living in the midst of our fellowmen, and showing practical interest in their welfare, can we hope each of us to become in some small measure the "salt of the earth," the "light of the world."
>
> But how can we accomplish this? First, by respecting the freedom of conscience and the essential freedom of the act of faith; secondly, by loyally accepting and respecting everything that is good and true in other religions; and lastly, by using spiritual means to reach our spiritual goal.[10]

The whole thrust of this remarkable letter is forward-looking and realistic in its church-state philosophy and in its practical directives for the Tanganyikan people. Distinction is made between *society* and the *state*, the latter being a living action in society directed to a limited end, the happiness of man in the temporal order. So conceived, the state owes no special privilege to Catholicism. The Church, in turn, claims no prerogative but profits by the creation of those social conditions of justice, order, and peace in which men are free to seek the truth and to fulfill their divine destiny.

Catholic ecclesiological history, in the view of a leading French theologian, has been characterized by an oscillating tension "between the two poles, Pope and Church."[11] We might ask ourselves, he suggests, whether

. . . the first of these poles has not completely absorbed the second: somewhat in the manner in which in the apostolic foundation of the

[10] *Ibid.*, p. 229.
[11] Yves M. J. Congar, O.P., "The Council, the Church, and the 'Others,'" *Cross Currents*, Summer, 1961, p. 248.

Church of Rome, Peter absorbed Paul. Will the Church be but the passive recipient of decisions transmitted with authority by its head, or will it again come alive, certainly not cut off from this visible head, but transmitting something to him as well? Will the life of the Church have a structure designed for monologue or one designed for dialogue?[12]

Certainly, one can agree that there is an abundance of material for dialogue on the crucial problem of a satisfactory formulation of a theology of religious toleration.[13] The urgency of the task was again underscored by the religious controversy in the 1960 American presidential election, as well as by the obviously universal reach of the contemporary drive for freedom in its manifold aspects. All over the globe today men are aspiring to an authentic personal freedom with economic, social, political, and religious dimensions. They are claiming religious liberty as an inviolable right of the autonomous individual conscience, a right open to all human beings and not equated with membership in any particular ethnic, racial, or faith group. Religious pluralism on the international and domestic scene is likely to remain an existential fact in the foreseeable future, even though for Catholics it is theologically inadmissible as an absolute ideal.

There is moreover a growing realization of the challenge to believers in God posed by a subtly aggressive atheism and a pervasive and decadent secularism. The widening arc of freedom may succeed in breaking down traditional barriers of prejudice and discrimination and lead to cooperative efforts by all who acknowledge that the universe, the nation, and the

---

[12] *Ibid.*

[13] Norman St. John-Stevas, "Catholicism and Religious Toleration: Some Notes Towards a Restatement of the Catholic Attitude to Religious Liberty in a Contemporary Pluralist Society," *Wiseman Review*, Summer, 1961, pp. 99–108.

individual stand under the sovereignty of God. The need of such a constructive enterprise is evidenced by the negative character of much of the current drive, directed as it is to the removal of restrictions and the release from institutional entanglements, with little appreciation of the concept of freedom as a positive empowerment, ultimately functional to man's last end. For those who accept the transcendental nature of religion, herein precisely lies the opportunity to shape its present historical form and stance so that it can best serve the highest interests of the whole human community.

The American Catholic Record

What do American Catholics think about the relationship between church and state? Are they satisfied with the First Amendment? Do they seek a privileged position for their Church in the legal structure of the land? The record of American Catholic attitudes and performance is the fairest indication of present and future intentions regarding the constitutional provision for church-state separation.[14]

The First Amendment grew out of the social contingencies of our colonial beginnings and our emergence as an independent nation. It embodies a characteristically American assertion of an authentic Christian principle—the distinction between church and state. It denies to government any competence in spiritual matters, and guarantees to the church untrammeled freedom to organize itself and pursue its mission without political interference. Thus Catholic citizens, both clerical and lay, have al-

[14] Edward Duff, S.J., "Church-State in the American Environment: An Historical and Legal Survey," *Social Order*, November, 1960, pp. 385–402.

ways unhesitatingly endorsed the religion clauses of the federal constitution. Likewise, the hierarchy, from John Carroll to the present day, have accepted and defended the American pattern of church-state relations. The first bishop of the United States declared openly: "We have all smarted heretofore under the lash of an established church, and shall therefore be on our guard against every approach towards it."[15] In a more positive vein, he continued: "Freedom and independence, acquired by the united efforts, and cemented with the mingled blood of Protestant and Catholic fellow citizens, should be equally enjoyed by all."[16]

Archbishop Karl J. Alter of Cincinnati, reflecting the best contemporary thinking, said in 1960:

> The fear that we as Catholics will use religious toleration here to gain the ascendancy in our country, and then, having achieved political hegemony, proceed to deprive our fellow citizens of freedom of speech in religion, freedom of conscience, or impose our convictions upon them willy-nilly, is utterly unwarranted by any doctrine of the Catholic Church, as well as by the consistent pronouncements of the American hierarchy. We seek no privileged status; we proclaim our full adherence to the provisions of the Constitution as of now as well as for the future.[17]

When Catholics fail to measure up to this high standard, they simply manifest a human problem of performance and not of credal compulsion.

A great deal of campaign literature on the question of the union of church and state dealt with abstractions, an amazing contradiction of the American penchant for practical, flesh-and-

[15] Quoted in John Tracy Ellis, "Church and State: An American Catholic Tradition," *Harper's*, November, 1953, p. 64.
[16] *Ibid.*
[17] Archbishop Karl J. Alter, "A Catholic President," *Sign*, July, 1960, pp. 14, 65.

blood realities. One suspects, however, that in this case "rigid" Catholic formulas were not so much the source of fresh anxiety as the refuge of those with a prior commitment to fear or bigotry. Protestant hesitation about entrusting political power to Catholics has psychological, sociological, and historical dimensions which cannot be ignored. There is a natural desire for reassurance at the highest level of the Church that what they see as the burgeoning "liberal" current in Catholic thought will not be submerged in a counterwave of reaction. This is a characteristic wish of even the most open-minded and sympathetic Protestant spokesmen and might well engage the attention of informed and articulate Catholics. Dr. Robert McAfee Brown, for example, speaking of Protestant fears about "Catholic power," observes:

> Here is where the Roman Catholic must likewise engage in an act of good will. His particular responsibility will be to see that the voices that offer a creative alternative to the "Spanish line" get a wider hearing both within his own church and outside. If he possesses such a voice, he must speak loudly enough so that his Protestant neighbors can hear. If he wields a pen he must not wield it for scholarly journals buried in seminary libraries, but for popular journals exposed on public newsstands. If he only knows that such voices exists, he must help to make their message more audible to both Protestants and Roman Catholics.[18]

A growing awareness of the diversity of Catholic opinion opens up vistas of further exploration and clarification. Curiously, it is no exaggeration to admit with an astute Jewish analyst the

> . . . distinct possibility of an unprecedented coalition of Catholic and Protestant right-fundamentalists in the 1960's. Only those who know little about the history of American Catholicism would assume that it is

[18] Robert McAfee Brown, *The Spirit of Protestantism*, New York, Oxford University Press, 1961, p. 166.

a monolithic community. Yet many factors suggest that the 1960's may see an even deeper division of American Catholics into warring ideological factions than has obtained at any time in the past.[19]

It is not without significance that the most vocal anti-Catholic spokesmen during the campaign came from the same reservoir of reaction as the consistent critics of the National Council of the Churches of Christ and of other liberal elements within Protestantism. Indeed, the heavy Catholic representation in the postelection tide of right-wing extremism augurs ill for a rational approach to the complex problems of the modern world. This phenomenon seems to cement bonds across religious lines among like-minded Catholics, Protestants, and Jews and to widen rifts within the respective faith groups. Evidently there is need for serious intramural dialogue between the divided segments of whatever church or synagogue. Precious little in the philosophy or program of the "radical right" commends itself to Catholic social thought, and even less to the genius of American democracy. A healthy pluralism is not well served by an intellectually underprivileged diet of extreme right or left. Allied with the ruptures of religious division, the disintegrative effect of such a polarization might be disastrous to the minimal consensus required by a political community.

DUAL ALLEGIANCE OF AMERICAN CATHOLICS

A second campaign charge against Catholics is the presumed burden of dual allegiance—to a Church whose supreme head

[19] Alan F. Westin, "The John Birch Society, Fundamentalism on the Right," *Commentary*, August, 1961, pp. 103–104.

is in a foreign country, and to a state whose prime purpose is promotion of the national interest. The supposed inevitable conflict between the two, it is alleged, will just as inevitably find Catholics opting for the Church over the state, the Pope over the President. To pose the problem solely in abstract terms is to negate in advance the possibility of a satisfactory response. Unwarranted even at this level, moreover, are both predictions. On the concrete existential plane, the twin presumptions must first be clothed in the particular garb of a given proposition or problem with the attendant relativities which will only then allow full scope for a prudential judgment. Catholics, like others, reach decisions by weighing the proximate in the light of the permanent, and are not provided with prepackaged solutions to every conceivable dilemma. They do not normally experience undue hardship in adhering to an authoritarian Church in religious matters and at the same time engaging freely with fellow citizens in political debate with the outcome subject to majority decision. Nor does the "hierarchy" stand in stern surveillance over the layman, influencing or dictating his thoughts, words, and actions. At the same time, there is ample room for considerable growth in genuine lay responsibility for temporal political matters. A sizable amount of campaign literature harped on the dangers of clerical control, and it could to some extent provide documentation for the felt need of adding a chapter called *De Laicis* to the 1870 Vatican Council's *Prima Constitutio de Ecclesia.*

Some of the sharpness might be removed from the edge of controversy over federal aid to education if the effort to obtain a share for parochial schools had originally been spearheaded by parents' groups instead of the hierarchy. Those who oppose the whole move as a threat to the public school system find support in a parallel trend to resist all intervention in the political sphere by an institutional church in its corporate capacity. Popular emphasis on individual rights and liberties minimizes the role of organized religion in bringing moral and theological principles to bear on social and political problems. Church activity, in this view, should be confined to instructing and forming lay leaders who would then be responsible for decisions which are at once morally tenable and politically relevant.

On the other hand, the case for the right of churches to give formal expression to the implications of their belief for governmental policy was cogently stated by Dean John C. Bennett of Union Theological Seminary in New York: "The American concept of church-state separation has never meant that churches and synagogues should not seek to influence legislation. On the contrary, they have a responsibility to keep the public conscience *instructed* and *disturbed*."[20]

It is to be hoped that churches and synagogues, instead of confronting one another as beleaguered units of countervailing power, will work out a permanently structured dialogue to carry on their shared concern for public well-being. The imaginative program of the National Conference of Christians and Jews on Religious Freedom and Public Affairs is a step in this direction. Launched in 1961, the main objectives of the four-year project, according to Conference President Dr. Lewis Webster Jones, are:

[20] John C. Bennett, "An Address to the Fall Delegate Assembly of the Manhattan Division of the Protestant Council," October, 1960, cited in De Albornoz, "Ecumenical Chronicle . . . ," p. 479.

1. To analyze the varied practical and theoretical problems involving political action and religious freedom;
2. to bring greater intellectual coherence and depth into interreligious relationships and public policy;
3. to lessen destructive conflict created by different religious approaches to social problems.[21]

Catholics, Protestants, and Jews who have been involved in NCCJ-sponsored dialogue groups in major cities across the nation have made major contributions to interreligious understanding and the harmonious resolution of trying tensions.

MORAL PRINCIPLES AND CIVIL LAW

The "conspiratorial" mentality lies behind much of the campaign literature which charged Catholics with habitually seeking to enact their own morality into the civil law and so impose it on the whole community. This was tagged as inherent in the totalitarianism of the Church and designed as one phase of a long-range plan to dominate the country and deprive non-Catholics of their liberties. The plot theory is obviously false, but the illusion dies hard. Moreover, history amply illustrates attempts by various religious groups to translate their distinctive moral convictions into the law of the land. Prohibition was one such instance, and the present birth-control statutes in Massachusetts and Connecticut are others. Currently there seems to be a growing consensus among our religious communities that restraint is called for in the area of civil legislation on such sensitive subjects as censorship, family morality, and medical ethics. Consciences differ in their understanding of the moral

[21] "New Project Will Study Interreligious Conflicts," *Catholic Reporter* (Kansas City, Mo.), July 14, 1961, p. 1.

aspects of these complex matters, and no single group can rightly use the state to impose its interpretations on others, even when it has the political power to do so. Society can and indeed should protect the shared moral ideas which are accepted by its citizens and which operate in its institutions. But the precise content of the consensus and the mode and moment for the exercise of the right by the government will depend upon the counsel of prudence regarding whether a law would be effective, enforceable, and productive of greater good than evil. Such judgments cannot be made on a priori grounds alone, apart from the concrete context,

Perhaps it is because they had so far to go that Catholics seem to have come a long way in the past several years in acknowledging the built-in limitations of the civil code as a means of eradicating moral evil. Hopefully there might now be some modification of the verdict, widely held as recently as 1958, that American Catholics are "a kind of vast pressure group, intent on restricting here, banning there and picketing everywhere."[22] At any rate, the search is on for other and more sophisticated and appropriate methods of translating ideals of truth and goodness into social reality.

PUBLIC FUNDS FOR CATHOLIC SCHOOLS

Public aid to parochial schools cropped up in campaign literature as an example of the persistent and relentless drive of the Church to dip into tax funds for partisan religious purposes in clear defiance of the constitutional principle of separation of

[22] James O'Gara, "Catholics and the Dialogue," *Commonweal*, May 30, 1958, p. 228.

49

church and state. The initial dip in the form of auxiliary services for Catholic school children, as the argument went, would be the camel's nose leading inevitably to a demand for direct aid to schools with the consequent weakening or destruction of the public educational system.

Postelection controversy over this most crucial church-state issue has been considerably more strident on both sides than was indicated in campaign material on the subject. Failure of the 87th Congress to pass a general federal aid to education measure cannot be blamed on the first Catholic President but on the deep-rooted disagreement over the status of public schools in our society. Have they a monopoly on "public education" which makes them the unique constitutional claimant of public funds? Is their unifying function endangered by a parallel system of privately conducted (perhaps government-aided) schools? What happens to the integrity of the First Amendment when separation of church and state is absolutized at the expense of the free exercise of religion? Are the adversaries of government aid to parochial schools equally sensitive to the implications for parental rights of stricter legal limitations on church-related education? These and like questions are prompting careful and extensive research and reassessment with results that should raise the level of public comprehension and perhaps indicate lines along which an acceptable solution can be sought. This is a prime need, since it involves whole theories of society and government, rights of parents, the moral and political welfare of the nation, and the very meaning of American pluralism.

The argument of those who favor channeling federal aid

to education through secular and sectarian schools is fair and persuasive at the level of theory and detached from human emotions, fears, and prejudices. But the politically explosive potential of such a proposal has contributed to the contemporary legislative stalemate. Basically, there are four focal points of the argument which merit attention.

First, the religious pluralism of the United States should be sufficiently flexible to admit the same freedom of expression in education as in other fields.[23] A program of government support for the public secular school alone ignores the economic exigencies of such freedom and ultimately inhibits its normal exercise. It is, in fact, a relic of the past, out of touch with the present and ill-adapted to the future of a dynamic society which requires pragmatic adjustments in the course of its development. The existential American religious pattern has outdistanced the thinking of those who would freeze into constitutional permanence a venerable nineteenth-century sociological model. Evidence that this point has gained some measure of acceptance, in regard to higher education at least, is apparent in the relatively noncontroversial nature of proposals to assist students at denominational colleges and universities. The same principles are applicable at elementary and secondary levels, though the factual circumstances of the two cases are somewhat different. In the first place, there is the compulsory aspect of elementary and secondary schooling in accordance with state law. Second, the present national need for college-trained men and women could in no wise be adequately met by public

[23] Justus George Lawler, "Federal Aid and Freedom," *Commonweal*, January 26, 1962, pp. 451–454.

institutions alone. Third, university religion courses are presumably primarily intellectual and informative rather than prescriptive and formative. Hence, proposals to assist higher education by grants, loans, and scholarships need not distinguish between secular and sectarian institutions to the same degree. The next step would be to find an acceptable way of helping students who are preparing for college. Some, in fact, make this claim:

> Since it is compulsory that all children obtain elementary education, and since the education which the state requires may be obtained in church-related schools, and since these are the sole schools which certain children may as a matter of conscience attend, and, finally, since these schools presently are educating millions of American children, therefore it would seem that the institutions performing this public task (or the children who therein fulfil their public obligation) should have a clearer claim for public funds than would institutions or students in higher education.[24]

A second facet of the argument embraced by partisans of sectarian school aid focuses on the nature and functions of these schools. The public service they render is amply documented by the number of children educated under conditions which measure up to the stiffest state requirements. Recent figures show a total student enrollment of 42,099,576 in all elementary and secondary schools, public and nonpublic.[25] Of this number, 5,287,230 are enrolled in Catholic elementary and secondary schools, which amounts to 12.56 percent of the total.

[24] National Catholic Welfare Conference, Legal Department, *The Constitutionality of the Inclusion of Church-Related Schools in Federal Aid to Education,* reprinted from "Analysis of 'Memorandum on the Impact of the First Amendment to the Constitution upon Federal Aid to Education,' Issued by the Department of Health, Education, and Welfare, March 28, 1961," *Georgetown Law Journal,* Winter, 1961, Annex B, p. 450.

[25] "Statistical Tables," in *ibid.,* Annex A, pp. 443–444.

Grants or loans for science, foreign language, English, or social studies training, for example, would not necessarily fall under any existing constitutional ban. On the contrary, Supreme Court decisions in this area as well as legislative enactments like the GI Bill suggest that much could be done to aid nonreligious subjects, given the will to do so.

Rather than being "divisive," schools which blend the sectarian with the secular attest the healthy diversity of a strong democracy whose true unity precludes an easy identification with rigid monolithic uniformity in the education of its youth. It is not clear, moreover, whether "merely mingling together or whether the mystique or the instruction of the public school produces a unifying effect, an effect which somehow is thought to be highly desirable."[26] In fine, the polemic for the "unity-producing function" of the single common school lacks convincing formulation as well as supporting evidence from historical experience. The specter of the public monopoly which might ensue from excessive economic penalties against the private sector in education should have little appeal to a people boastful of a tradition of academic freedom and jealous of the right to unfettered intellectual inquiry.

Third, there is the place of parental rights both in Catholic social thought and in American constitutional law. In the 1929 encyclical *Divini illius magistri* (the Christian Education of Youth), Pius XI stated the basic premise:

The family therefore holds directly from the Creator the mission and hence the right to educate the offspring, a right inalienable because inseparably joined to a strict obligation, a right anterior to any right

[26] Robert F. Drinan, S.J., "Should the State Aid Private Schools?", *Social Order,* June, 1961, p. 249.

whatever of civil society and of the state, and therefore inviolable on the part of any power on earth.[27]

In *Meyer v. Nebraska* (262 U.S. 390), 1923, the United States Supreme Court made it clear that the Constitution protects the rights of the teacher, the parent, and the child against unwarranted intrusion by the state. The pivotal decision of *Pierce v. Society of Sisters* (268 U.S. 150), 1925, involved a more explicit rejection of state monopoly in education and a stronger vindication of parental rights:

> The fundamental theory of liberty upon which all governments in this Union repose excludes any general power of the state to standardize its children by forcing them to accept instruction from public teachers only. The child is not the mere creature of the state; those who nurture him and direct his destiny have the right, coupled with the high duty, to recognize and prepare him for additional obligations.[28]

The Meyer and Pierce cases both underscore the constitutional protection of individual rights in education, especially those of parents. Quite obviously, a pattern of federal spending for public schools only would hinder and possibly destroy the freedom of parents to choose church-related education for their children if it reached such proportions as to require the cessation of all other kinds of education in the land.

A fourth and final point of the argument turns on the constitutionality of federal aid to parochial schools. Careful scrutiny of the relevant aspects of constitutional law has so far yielded incompatible and even conflicting opinions which are presently vying for popular support, pending a settlement of the matter by the Court. Private nonreligious schools are less vulnerable

[27] Pius XI, *Divini illius magistri*, in Joseph Husslein, S.J., ed., *Social Wellsprings*, Milwaukee, Bruce, 1942, II, 97.
[28] Quoted in *Georgetown Law Journal*, Winter, 1961, pp. 431–432.

to exclusion than their parochial counterparts because of the controversy over the meaning of the "establishment of religion" clause of the First Amendment. Broadly interpreted, as in *Everson* v. *Board of Education* (330 U.S. 1), 1947, it would rule out aid of any kind to religion in any guise. Moderately construed, it would permit a policy of aid to education in church-related schools in proportion to the public function therein performed, thus safeguarding the prior right to the free exercise of religion. To date, there is nothing definite in constitutional law which prohibits every type of government assistance to religious schools or to parents who choose such schools for their children. Still to be judicially clarified is the precise meaning of "state action" in the sense of that "public action" which is eligible for government support as well as subject to government regulation.

No simple single program of providing justice in the tangled area of church-state relations in education seems forthcoming in the immediate future. There are, however, some suggestions to be pondered as we devote time and talent to the task of resolving a troublesome problem: (1) concern for the full integrity of the First Amendment—the "free exercise" as well as the "establishment of religion" clause; (2) sensitiveness on the part of all groups to the requirements of the common good in the political order; (3) self-limitation in the use of power to implement by legal enactment any particular vision of the "good society"; (4) recognition and respect for the traditional place of religious values in American society; and (5) willingness to settle for a pragmatic solution acceptable to the great majority though fully satisfactory to none.

WEALTH, POWER, AND CORRUPTION

A last category of campaign charges against Catholicism was the general one of wealth, power, and corruption. Horror tales of convents and monasteries were the burden of numerous sensational tracts authored for the most part by misfits who had fled the priesthood or sisterhood. Geared to the lowest level of literacy, these anti-Catholic diatribes satisfied an unabashed bigotry commensurate with the stepped-up output of leading publishing houses. Cyrus Osterhus of Minneapolis, the largest producer of the tracts, estimated that the demand for anti-Catholic literature more than doubled after the presidential nomination. He anticipated a sales increase from 25,000,000 in 1959 to 35,000,000 in 1960.[29] The pieces were probably most effective among those already committed to opposing a Catholic President, though there is some evidence of a reverse effect in favor of the Democratic nominee. Whatever the impact on vote totals, it is important to recognize in this sizable burst of hostility "a warning that in the mass electorate the potential for social friction on these bases is far from dead."[30]

For Catholics, this might well serve as a spur to inner spiritual renewal, concern for the public image of the Church, and attention to the thoughts, feelings, and aspirations of all segments of society.

[29] John Wicklein, "Anti-Catholic Groups Closely Cooperate in Mail Campaign to Defeat Kennedy," *New York Times*, October 17, 1960, p. 24C.

[30] Philip E. Converse, "Religion and Politics: The 1960 Elections," paper delivered at the Annual Meeting of the American Sociological Association, St. Louis, August-September, 1961, p. 56.

CHAPTER THREE

Toward a Realized Pluralism

WHAT are the lessons for American democracy from the sharply debated religious issue in the 1960 presidential campaign? First of all, no great perspicacity is required to recognize that the election of a Catholic President constitutes a minimal and chiefly symbolic victory for a realized pluralism. It by no means marks the end of controversy and conflict. An analysis of campaign material shows that, religiously, we do not even know one another. To correct this defect, a three-part approach merits consideration. First, there should be more extensive and inclusive involvement in *dialogue* in order to rid ourselves of the caricatures which persist. The aim, at this stage, would be to present, ponder, and probe views about religion's relationship to the ambiguities of politics. It would mean an encounter between people who think it worthwhile to get to know each other on a person-to-person basis. Current efforts, it has been observed, are largely confined to "religious professionals and intellectuals, without reaching very deeply into the lay communities."[1] Broader representation is thus needed to ensure

[1] William Lee Miller, "What Hopes and What Misgivings Do You Entertain Regarding the Currently Emerging Religious Dialogue in America?", *America*, January 14, 1961, p. 460. Also, Dr. C. Emanuel Carlson, executive director of the Baptist Joint Committee on Public Affairs, makes the point that most instances of dialogue have been theoretic or theological rather than administrative: "Clericalism is obviously not dead, but ecclesiastical formulations may be far behind the tendencies

57

better results. Preparation for this kind of experience should start with high-school and college students and be carried over to the adult level by means of regular discussion groups, appropriately structured in accordance with local conditions.

Second, this initial personal confrontation should move on to organized, full, and frank debate on concrete social and political issues which concern the national and international common good, for instance, the complex problem of population growth —facts, determinants, consequences, and morally licit methods of dealing with it. Public understanding would profit by listening to and participating in a spirited intellectual exchange, provided that there was real *listening* and genuine *participation*. A concerted educational effort seems called for to make such an opportunity as universal as possible. Our differences have to do not only with the substantive content of diverse theological traditions but with whole systems of thought and methods of expression. Anyone who has had a chance for the kind of enrichment achieved through a dialogue in depth will be better equipped to comprehend and cope with the range of opinions on a particular point which is a normal characteristic of a vital democracy.

Third, public policy decisions will ultimately be shaped in the give-and-take of the legislative forum which Americans readily acknowledge as the assigned arena of power struggles.

---

of our age with reference to these shifts. . . . In brief, when viewed in terms of level of participation at present, there is little in the current dialogue that has significance for the political pressure of ecclesiastical bodies. Such signs of encouragement as appear are now monologue rather than dialogue. Whether they can gain influence to become dialogue is an open question" ("Levels of the Dialogue," *Chaplain,* October, 1960, pp. 21, 23).

Hence, to accuse one side or another of using pressure tactics is to recite the obvious. Hopefully, there would be fewer accusations against Catholics of un-American aspirations, foreign-dominated ambitions, and clerical dictation if the first two phases of this program were carefully implemented. This is admittedly a long-range assignment.

One cannot escape the conclusion that in the whole field of intergroup relations, the United States has a great deal of unfinished business which invites the country to a more purposeful endeavor than presently exists. The alarm of the religious-minded over the steady erosion of a cherished consensus about the place of God in the public life of the nation is matched by the determination of nonbelievers to win legal recognition of their claim to full membership in the pluralist American society. The continued success of their efforts may well prod the partisans of religion into the kind of unity predicated on shared goals and common undertakings, rather than an ideological agreement about abstract principles. Such a pragmatic enterprise seems called for if this generation is to strengthen and pass on the twin pillars of the American heritage: acceptance of religion as indispensable to genuine democracy, and respect for religious freedom and the pluralist tradition of dissent.

APPENDIX A

Campaign Pieces

THE FOLLOWING list of items circulated during the 1960 campaign was compiled from the material in the files of the Fair Campaign Practices Committee, 45 East 65th Street, New York 12, New York, and of the National Conference of Christians and Jews, 43 West 57th Street, New York 19, New York. Included in this section, along with booklets, pamphlets, and similar pieces, are (1) local and special-interest media which published an issue, article, or separate item and (2) certain organizations and individuals who printed and distributed statements, letters, sermons, and the like in connection with the campaign. The alphabetical arrangement is somewhat arbitrary, since some of the items are untitled and others defy consistent classification on any single basis. The list is intended as a handy reference for readers who may be interested in concrete examples of the campaign pieces.

THE ABAREE (monthly magazine), ed. by A. O. Hart, 207 North Washington Rd., Enid, Okla.; editorial office: 2522½ North Monroe St., Enid, Okla.; October, 1960. Claims that a Catholic President would not really be the head of the state because he would be subject to the Pope. By electing a Catholic President, we would make the Pope the head of the state, and this would endanger peace with Russia. We should not permit ourselves to become involved in war with Russia to further the aims of the Catholic Church.

ABOLISH THE NUNNERIES AND SAVE THE GIRLS, by Rev. L. J. King, Kane Ministry, Inc., 217 Woodland Ave., Merchantville, N.J. What life would be like in America under a dictatorship.

Actions Speak Louder than Words. Car stickers urging votes against Masons and Shriners. Apparently a Catholic piece—local circulation in Minnesota.

Advent Christian Witness (monthly), October, 1960, p. 8: "Which Way, America?," by Raymond M. Beecraft. Insists that the great unanswered question in the minds of thousands of voters is: "Can the unofficial position of Roman Catholic Leaders regarding separation of church and state supersede that of the long-standing and irrevocable, official position of the Church?" Suggests that Senator Kennedy request Vatican endorsement of the position he has taken publicly.

Am I Really a Religious Bigot? (16-page mimeographed pamphlet). Opposed to Senator Kennedy solely because he is a member of the Roman Catholic Church. Reasons:

1. Roman Catholicism is antidemocratic.
2. Roman Catholicism is anti-public school.
3. Roman Catholicism is anti-religious liberty.
4. Roman Catholicism is anti-freedom of thought.
5. Roman Catholicism desires political domination.
6. Roman Catholicism is anti-American law.
7. The Roman Catholic Church is ready to claim the U.S. for the Pope.

America Is a Catholic Country (4-page pamphlet), pub. by the Catholic Committee for Historical Truth, J. J. O'Connor, chmn. A smooth, bragging presentation of the overwhelming Catholic influence in the United States from its earliest days. Calculated to antagonize Protestants and other Americans. This was a clever piece of hate literature—a hoax—since the Catholic Committee for Historical Truth was nonexistent.

America Withers (4-page leaflet), by F. P. Wortman, reprinted from *Progressive World*, Box 27, Clifton, N.J. Alleges that the Roman Catholic political machine is set up to undermine this country. The wealth of the Church is enormous, the sacerdotal tyranny and lawlessness an outrage.

AMERICAN BAPTISTS AND OTHER PROTESTANTS, WAKE UP! (2 mimeographed sheets), from W. Earle Smith, exec., American

Baptist Union of San Francisco Bay Cities, August, 1960. A series of excerpts showing the dangers of a Roman Catholic President. Claims not to be against Catholicism as a religious faith but as a totalitarianism with a world organization centering in a foreign land and denying the right of any religion to exist outside its own hierarchy.

AMERICAN CAPSULE NEWS (weekly newsletter), ed. and pub. by Morris A. Bealle, 919 18th St., Washington 6, D.C., October 8, 1960: "John F. Kennedy—Catholic or Red?" by Emanuel Josephson. Asserts that Kennedy and his supporters have stirred up the religious controversy to hide the far uglier fact that Kennedy is in reality "a dedicated Red who assiduously courts Communist support."

AMERICAN CHRISTIAN REVIEW, pub. by B. K. Sommer, Box 23102, Indianapolis, Ind., June, 1960. Warns of the Roman Church's aim to seize power in the U.S. by slipping in thousands who are subject to papal power through a relaxation of the immigration laws. Cites a 1950 instance of Kennedy's yielding to "clerical pressure" by not attending the gathering in Philadelphia for the dedication of a chapel to honor the four chaplains lost on the *Dorchester* in World War II.

AMERICAN COUNCIL OF CHRISTIAN CHURCHES, 15 Park Row, New York 38, N.Y. A letter, "Dear Christian Friends and Brothers," by Herman Mierins urges people to preach and fight against the election of a Catholic President because of "Catholic imperialism," which seeks to gain secular power over the whole world.

AMERICAN HUMANIST ASSOCIATION, Yellow Springs, Ohio. A statement by its Committee on Church and State notes that the two big issues, if Kennedy is nominated, will be (1) appropriation of public money for sectarian schools and (2) birth-control freedom.

AMERICAN INDIAN LIBERATION CRUSADE, INC., Rev. Henry E. Hedrick, pres. and dir., 1059 South Hope St., Los Angeles 15, Cal. A letter to pastors alerting them to Catholic persecution of the American Indians and to the consequent threat to the freedom of all Americans if Kennedy is elected.

AMERICAN PEOPLE BETRAYED (1-page mimeographed sheet), pub. by *Ripsaw* (*q.v.*), P.O. Box 3002, Station B, South Bend, Ind. Quotes, out of context, from Boniface VIII, Leo XIII, Pius IX, and Pius XII to show that the Catholic Church is a foreign dictatorial power which does not believe in separation of church and state.

THE AMERICAN PROTEST ed. by Thomas E. Little, official organ of the American Protestant Defense League, Inc., 350 West 26th St., New York 1, N.Y., April, 1960, pp. 3–4: "The Real Issue: Why a Practising Roman Catholic Is Not Fit To Be President." A letter from Angelo di Domenica, retired Baptist minister, West Sand Lake, N.Y., stressing the absolute servility of all Roman Catholics to Church authority.

American Women Are Slaves to Catholic Dogmas (leaflet), by James H. Johnson, pub. by Guardians of the Constitution, Box 75673 Sanford Sta., Los Angeles 5, Cal. Theme: the slavery imposed on Catholic women by the Church's stand against artificial birth control.

America's Need: A New Protestant Awakening (folder), pub. by the Georgia Bible Institute, Athens, Ga. Claims that there is no freedom of religion for the average Roman Catholic in America today.

Are Protestants Intolerant and Misinformed? (1-page flyer), pub. by Knights of Christ, Inc., Box 1651, Long Beach, Cal. Cites the fact that the U.S. is 80 percent non-Catholic and enjoys freedom of religion. There is no country on earth where Romanism has prospered as in the U.S. There is no Catholic country which grants the same freedom to Protestants.

Arkansas Baptist News Magazine, ed. by Erwin L. McDonald, 401 West Capitol, Little Rock, Ark., July 2, 1960, pp. 4–5: "Should a Catholic Be Elected President?" Answer that no Baptist can consistently support a Catholic for office any more than a Catholic can exercise his own judgment in discharging the duties of office apart from the will of the Catholic hierarchy.

The Aryan Knights Ku Klux Klan: White Folk News (weekly newspaper), ed. by Horace Sherman Miller, G.H.Q., Box 5062, Waco, Tex., June 1, 1960. An impassioned advocacy of separation of church and state, and a warning of the dangers of Roman Catholicism.

September 14, 1960. The Roman Catholic stand is to try to make Americans think that they will not be subservient to any Pope.

Ashland Avenue Baptist (newspaper), ed. by Clarence Walker, 163 North Ashland Ave., Lexington, Ky. Special issues dealing with "the most vital question before the American people today."

May 6, 1960: "Why I Am Afraid of a Roman Catholic President," by C. Walker. The main reason is that religious liberty is for Catholics only.

August 5, 1960: "Religious Freedom—The Church—The State and Senator Kennedy," and "Religious Freedom Won at a Terrible Price."

August 19, 1960: "Roman Catholicism—Politically."

September 9, 1960. A vicious issue, claiming that Kennedy owes allegiance to a foreign power, the Roman Catholic Church, which is dedicated to the destruction of our form of government and to the overthrow of our way of life.

September 16, 1960: "Why I Cannot Vote for Senator Kennedy."

September 23, 1960: "The Catholic State."

October 14, 1960: "The Struggle for the First Amendment to the Constitution."

Augusta Courier (weekly newspaper), ed. by Rev. V. Harris, September 26, 1960: "Strictly Personal." Links Kennedy to "big government spending" and hostility to white racial supremacy.

Awake! (periodical tract), pub. by Watchtower Bible and Tract Society of New York, Inc., special issue of October 8, 1960:

"The Catholic Church in the Twentieth Century." Charges against Catholicism include: (1) the Church is opposed to Bible reading because many Church teachings are not in the Bible; (2) the Catholic Church does not favor separation of church and state and freedom, as evidenced in, for instance, the *Syllabus* and the May 18, 1960, *Osservatore Romano;* (3) the Church was responsible for World Wars I and II since it supported Nazis and Fascists; (4) the Church is not effective against communism, as proved by the large numbers in "Catholic" lands; and (5) the Church is too lax on morals, one example being her attitude toward gambling.

BAPTIST CHURCH, Durham, N.C. (16 mimeographed pages). This item explains why religious faith is important, and states the case against Catholicism by a series of quotes. Introduction by Douglas M. Branch, Biblical recorder.

Baptists, Roman Catholics and Religious Freedom (12-page leaflet), by Henlee H. Barnette, pub. by the Sunday School Board of the Southern Baptist Convention, Nashville, Tenn. Claims that the two great forces threatening religious freedom in the U.S. are the Roman Catholic hierarchy and the Russian Communist Party. Indictment of the Catholic Church: (1) it seeks state support; (2) it suppresses other churches—witness Spain and South America; (3) it opposes public schools; (4) it resorts to boycotting movies and censoring books and newspapers; (5) it opposes mixed marriages; and (6) Catholic countries are more vulnerable to communism than are Protestant countries.

Beacon Light Herald (monthly magazine), ed. by William Kullgren, Box 756, Atascadero, Cal., June 1960: excerpts from anti-Catholic pieces published elsewhere—"The Pope for President," "How Loyal Is Kennedy?", "Why I Am Afraid of a Roman Catholic President"; August, 1960: "Pope to Stay in Politics," "Catholics Are Forbidden to Attend Any Protestant Service," "Why Not a Roman Catholic President?", "Reject a Catholic for President." All these articles are anti-Catholic.

Behind the Dictators, by L. H. Lehmann, pub. by Agora Publishing Co., 120 Liberty St., New York 6, N.Y., first published 1942. Claims to be a factual analysis of the relationship between Nazi-Fascism and Roman Catholicism.

Berean Banner, ed. by Dr. R. D. Ingle, pastor, Berea Baptist Church, P.O. Box 3252, Jacksonville, Fla., October 14, 1960: "How the Roman Catholic Church Would Change the Constitution." A contrast between the Supreme Court position and the alleged "Catholic" position.

"The Famous Knights of Columbus Oath," by Harvey H. Springer. Warns that Rome never changes and that Kennedy is a loyal son of Rome.

Berean Messenger (2-page mimeographed sheet), from Dr. Ivan E. Olsen, pastor, Berean Fundamental Church, P.O. Box 549, North Platte, Neb., September 27, 1960. Laments the cry of bigotry against Protestants who say anything about the evils of Roman Catholicism. Numerous instances of Catholic intolerance, for example, in Spain and other Catholic-dominated countries. Doubts that it would be possible for a Roman Catholic President to be fair, in appointments, for instance, because of the terrific pressure which would be put on him.

The Bible Friend (8-page monthly newspaper), pub. by Osterhus Publishing Co., 4500 West Broadway, Minneapolis 22, Minn., November, 1960: "A Roman Catholic for President?—No," by Jack Odom. A letter to the editor.

Blessing Letter (4-page periodical letter), by William L. Blessing, founder and pastor, House of Prayer for all People, Inc., P.O. Box 837, Denver 1, Col., November, 1960. Warns of the powerful Roman Catholic organization, wealthy and gaining power in the U.S. Non-Catholics must stand together to prevent the Pope from controlling the White House and America from becoming a Fascist state.

Can a Man Be a Loyal Roman Catholic and a Good President of the United States? (leaflet), by Rev. W. A. Criswell. Excerpts from a recent sermon by Reverend Criswell with the clear implication that the answer is no.

Candidate Kennedy and the Catholic Church (26-page booklet), by Vernon C. Grounds, Ph.D., 1500 East 10th Ave., Denver 18, Col. Singles out one factor in the coming election as crystal clear: "Woven into the fabric of the Catholic faith is a definite political philosophy. That philosophy is antagonistic to and irreconcilable with the system of government our chief executive is sworn to maintain. A good Catholic therefore cannot conscientiously serve as president of the United States." Thus, if Mr. Kennedy repudiates the attitude of his Church, he is a poor Catholic and if he declines to repudiate it, he is a poor presidential risk.

The Capital Call (8-page newspaper), pub. by P. A. Hrobak, Box 150, Middletown, Pa., November 1, 1960: "National Elections, 1960: Bigotry Still Is a Big Issue," by P. A. Hrobak. This appears to be an example of reverse bigotry. Hrobak claims that the three most common indictments against the Catholic Church which turn up in books and literature are (1) the Catholic position on toleration is simply a program of political expediency; (2) toleration for Catholics has the status of defined dogma; (3) the program of the Catholic Church contains ominous threats to the United States, especially if Catholics ever become a majority.

The Capital Voice (8-page monthly newspaper), ed. by Dale Crowle, Evangelist, Box 1, Washington 4, D.C., September, 1960: "Thinking Out Loud" (editorial column). Mr. Crowle expresses a friendly attitude toward American Catholics but deep concern about the Vatican program for the control of America as blueprinted in the papal encyclicals with their insistence on the establishment of religion, that is, the Catholic religion. The election of John Kennedy would be a step towards this system.

October, 1960: "Thinking Out Loud." Finds Kennedy's statements to the Houston ministers in direct conflict with the unswerving position of the Roman Catholic hierarchy. Perhaps he was given permission to make them. If not, he surely risks excommunication.

Captive Schools (folder), by C. Stanley Lowell, pub. by Protestants and Other Americans United, 1633 Massachusetts Ave., N.W., Washington 6, D.C. (see *Church and State*). Reveals the fact that an "astounding institution," the captive school, exists in at least twenty-two states. It is a public school that has been taken over by the Roman Catholic Church and is operated as one of its own parish schools. Such schools violate citizens' religious rights as guaranteed by the First and Fourteenth Amendments to the Federal Constitution, and are often in defiance of state laws.

The Catholic Challenger (8-page newspaper), ed. by W. L. King, June, 1960: "Are American Catholics Different?", by H. H. Springer. The U.S. Constitution calls for separation of church and state, but the Vatican has denounced this time and time again. The Catholic Church believes that civil authority should be used to compel obedience to her teachings. She believes that Catholic education should be supported by tax funds, and that *all* children, Catholic and non-Catholic alike, should be compelled to attend schools under the supervision of the Roman Catholic Church. Mr. Springer thinks that textbooks for Catholic schools, free bus transportation, and so on are all violations of the First Amendment.

August, 1960: "A New Roman Catholic Plan to Make America the Land of Mary for the Pope," by Herbert B. Reed; "Beware of Catholicism," by A. L. Vess, expressing alarm over the political possibilities of a cruel, deceitful Roman Catholic becoming President of the United States; "Can the United States of America Afford a Catholic President?", by Lonnie King.

A Catholic Constitution for America (40-page booklet), by John J. U. Arrien, 1804 South McPherrin Ave., Monterey Park, Cal., 1960. Sets forth the allegedly basic truths of a "Catholic Constitution" for America, wherein the Church would control the whole of life. Based on a series of quotes taken out of context from *Immortale Dei, Humani generis* (mistakenly called *Humanum genus*), Ryan and Millar's *State and*

68

Church, and other works. Insists that freedom of conscience, worship, teaching, speech, and the press are all endangered by Catholic teaching, which condemns the lay state and all liberal governments.

Catholic Political Power vs. Religious Liberty (leaflet), by Rev. Dennis J. Brown, P.O. Box 948, Riverside, Cal., August, 1960. Eight reasons for not voting for a Roman Catholic:
1. U.S. Constitution.
2. We believe in separation of church and state.
3. Closing of Protestant churches, as in Spain.
4. Infallibility claimed by the Pope.
5. Martyrs—the Catholic killing of Protestants.
6. The Roman Church gives voting orders.
7. Catholic educational teaching, for example, that the Church is the divinely appointed teacher.
8. Political rulers—contradictions between Catholic teaching and major policy decisions on governmental matters.

A Catholic for President (leaflet), radio message by Dr. Clarence R. Sands, pastor, First Baptist Church, San Jose, Cal., May, 1960. Expresses opposition to the total religious system and warns of the danger of clerical pressure.

A Catholic for President????? (leaflet), sermon by Reggie Thomas, First Church of Christ, Catlin, Ill., August 28, 1960. Notes the apparent contradictions between Catholic canon law and American civil law, and yet the former is obligatory for every Roman Catholic. Canons 731, 1325, 1557, 684, 1160, 1179, and 1013 especially are cited. Mr. Thomas sets forth three main views with regard to church-state issues:
1. State over church is the view held by Nazis and Communists.
2. The view held by Roman Catholics: church over state. This is a twentieth-century reality in the countries where the Church has power.
3. The Protestant view is that God and conscience rule both church and state.

Catholic or President (9-page pamphlet), by Harry F. Borleis, 6602

Alta Ave., Baltimore 6, Md. Asserts that a Catholic cannot become President and remain a true Catholic, for the oath of office conflicts with canon law. Reprinted as a 12-page pamphlet and distributed to delegates at the nominating conventions. Author knows little of canon law and transfers concepts to U.S. laws inappropriately.

A Catholic President Can Mean Vatican Control of America (4-page leaflet), distributed by Protestant Action, P.O. Box 8661, Los Angeles, Cal.

A Catholic President? The Predicament (16-page pamphlet), by Carl S. Meyer, pub. by Concordia Publishing House, St. Louis, Mo. Asserts truly that the question of a Roman Catholic candidate for President is a serious one for Catholics and Protestants alike, in view of the history and pronouncements of the Roman Church. For example, "What will happen if a Roman Catholic is elected president? Can a good citizen vote for someone as head of the government of this country whose allegiance is pledged to the head of the Vatican State? Will the Roman Catholic Church try to gain advantages for herself through a Roman Catholic president? Would he be subject to undue pressure and ecclesiastical discipline?" (p. 2).

The Catholic State (12-page booklet), by Norman H. Wells, pub. by Central Baptist Church, 2608 Kemper Lane, Cincinnati, Ohio. Sources for the views herein expressed: (1) writings of the Catholic Church; (2) the historical record of Catholic performance in countries where Catholicism has prevailed. Argument: Catholics believe that all authority comes from God, and since the Roman Catholic Church and the Pope alone are the voice of God, then it becomes necessary for the government to accept the Roman Catholic Church as the final authority on all matters which it deems spiritual. There are serious points of difference between the theories of government preferred and promoted by the Roman Catholic Church and the U.S. government. For example, Catholics believe that our government should make a public profession of religion,

70

and that that religion should be the Roman Catholic; they also believe that our laws should stop granting equal rights to all religions.

Catholicism—Religion—The Presidency—Commonsense (brochure), by Luther A. Smith, 33° Sovereign Grand Commander, reprinted from *The New Age,* official organ of the Supreme Council 33° Ancient and Accepted Scottish Rite of Freemasonry, Southern Jurisdiction, U.S. of A., 1733 Sixteenth St., N.W., Washington 9, D.C., February, 1960. Points to the great gulf between (1) the government and the ideology of the Vatican, which is a church-state under the autocratic control of the Pope, and (2) the system of free institutions established by the Founding Fathers under which the people are the sovereigns and enjoy the blessings of civil and religious liberty.

Catholicism on Trial (4-page pamphlet), by Ethel Meadows, pub. by Full Salvation Tract Society, Hanover, Pa. Directed to a criticism of Catholicism as a religion, not as a political system.

The Central Issue Concerning a Catholic for President (leaflet), part of a sermon by Pastor Marcus Gaston, Calvary Assembly, Inglewood, Cal., reprinted from *The Pentecostal Evangel,* 434 West Pacific St., Springfield, Mo., October 2, 1960. Claims that Romanism is more than a religion—that it is an "aggressive, militant political body, with the avowed intention of usurping control of government in every country possible." The laity are the victims of an authoritarian structure in which all matters of policy and dogma are determined at the top. The history of the Roman Catholic Church shows that it has always claimed to be the only true Church, with the right to restrict or destroy "error." A result of electing a Catholic President would be to enhance the political power of the Church in the U.S. through appointments of Catholics to key positions in state and national governments. There would soon follow the official recognition of the Catholic Church as the one Church above all America. Roman Catholicism and communism are equally menacing for freedom of worship.

A Challenge to Senator John Kennedy (tract), pub. by Freedom Tracts, P.O. Box 1504, Altadena, Cal., August, 1960. Opines that no President of the U.S. can be a loyal American and a loyal Roman Catholic, according to the standard set by the Roman Catholic Church. Senator Kennedy should decide to whom he owes his first allegiance—to the Church or to the Constitution.

Christian Heritage (magazine), pub. by Christ's Mission (an organization of former priests and monks), Stuart P. Garner, exec. dir., Robert G. Hawley, bus. mgr., 369 Carpenter Ave., Sea Cliff, L.I., N.Y., November, 1960: "Why I left the Roman Catholic Church," by Jacques Montas. An ex-priest claims that the doctrines and principles of government of the Roman Catholic Church are in direct conflict with progressive civilization. It does not really believe in church-state separation. If it allows some toleration, this is a matter of expediency, not a right. The author's experience was gained in Haiti, his native land, where he found the Church interfering in politics.

"A Critique of Authority in Roman Catholicism," by Dr. Bernard Ramm. Finds that the Roman Catholic Church has corrupted the revelation of God, especially through its doctrine of papal infallibility.

"Roman Catholic Missions in Latin America," by Francis J. Kieda. Notes the surge of evangelical Protestantism in nominally Catholic Latin America, thus making for freedom of worship. This surge has sparked a reaction by the Roman Church, for example, in the Papal Volunteer Program. The Church of Rome lost its position of leadership largely because of indifference to the basic social and economic needs of the people.

Church Herald and Holiness Banner, Overland Park, Kan., July 7, 1960: "How Will You Stand Come This November?" Fourteen questions and answers showing incompatibility be-

72

tween Catholicism and American democracy, especially with regard to religious liberty.

The Church Speaks (monthly), ed. by A. Word and Stewart Baker, 550 N.E. 76th Ave., Portland, Ore., September, 1960: "A General Warns," by Brig. Gen. Herbert C. Holdridge. A letter to our government pointing out that the Catholic Church is set and sworn to outlaw the Constitution of the U.S. It is a foreign-dominated dictatorship whose absolute orders are carried down to every Roman Catholic in the U.S., who, in turn, must become party to the subversion of our Constitution.

Church and State (monthly review), pub. by Protestants and Other Americans United for the Separation of Church and State, 1633 Massachusetts Ave., Washington 6, D.C., September, 1960, pp. 1, 5: "Church-State Issue Will Figure Importantly in 1960 Presidential Election Campaign," by Glenn L. Archer, executive director of POAU. Mr. Archer says that if the Catholic hierarchy would come out in pronouncement and in practice for the equality of creeds before the law, against tying church and state together, and against federal aid to parochial schools, then they would sweep away much of the anxiety that exists over electing a man like Kennedy to the White House. The core of Archer's concern is the desire of the Roman Catholic hierarchy to carve out a special place for the Church in American society.

POAU is a nonprofit educational organization, incorporated in 1948 in Washington, D.C. POAU works to keep church and state separate—"as the Constitution says they should be, and as the Supreme Court says they must be." The POAU program includes education and legal action. Along with *Church and State* and the specific publications listed throughout Appendix A, this group also publishes *Church-State Digest*, a digest of articles in *Church and State*.

The Coming Presidential Election (16 mimeographed pages), by Pastor Fred Nader, First Baptist Church, Sanford Ave. and Union St., Flushing, N.Y.

Part I: "The Religious Issue." Cites the bad record of the Catholic Church on the subject of separation of church and state (as in Argentina, Paraguay). Asserts that Roman Catholics believe that the Pope is the Vicar of Christ, the personal representative of Christ on earth. The Church is the Kingdom of Christ, and the Pope and the Church have the right to incorporate under their jurisdiction national and international governments, thus bringing all authority under the sway of Christ. The political implications are phenomenal if the basic philosophy of Rome is assumed. To qualify as a candidate for the U.S. presidency, a Catholic would have to separate himself from the Roman concept and control in order to support the American concept of church-state separation. He should be willing to work for the religious freedom of all in non-Protestant countries as well as to promote and protect the freedoms of all in this country.

Part II: "Separation of Church and State Issue." States frankly how confusing to Protestants are the contrasting views held by Catholics regarding church-state separation. Sees as the official Catholic view, never repudiated by Rome or revised by American Catholics, the statement in *Civiltà Cattolica* (April, 1948): "The Roman Catholic Church, convinced through its divine prerogative of being the only true church, must demand *the right of freedom for herself alone,* because such a right can only be possessed by truth, never by error." Other religions will not be allowed to propagate false doctrine; consequently, "in a state where the majority of the people are Catholic, the Church will require that legal existence be denied to error, and that if religious minorities actually exist, they shall have only a *de facto* existence without opportunity to spread their beliefs."

Pastor Nader asks in conclusion whether American Catholic views which are not those of *Civiltà* are heretical by their own standard of unity and infallibility.

COMMITTEE FOR AMERICAN FREEDOMS, Box 1293, Grand Central Station, New York 17, N.Y. A letter, "Dear Voter," by D.

74

Margaret McCarter, dated November 1, 1960, warns that the Kennedy machine, like that of Tammany, is dominated by Roman Catholicism, an aggressive, militant political body that has the intention of getting control of the government. Thus, the decision in this most crucial election is whether to jeopardize our democratic traditions and the American way of life, or retain these principles and ideals. In making this decision, voters should remember that wherever Roman Catholicism gains the ascendancy, it dominates and controls the politics of the country.

COMMITTEE FOR HUMAN DIGNITY, William Levy, chmn., 46 Fort Washington Ave., New York 32, N.Y. A leaflet suggests a link between Joe Kennedy and Hitler and unfriendliness to the Jews.

COMMON SENSE (anti-Communist newspaper), ed. by Conde McGinley, pub. by Christian Educational Association, 530 Chestnut St., Union, N.J., June 15, 1960: "Kennedy's Marxist Record." Behind Kennedy stands the Jewish organizational bloc which will take our country if Kennedy wins.

The Convert (monthly magazine), ed. by Jos. Zacchello, D.D., pub. by American Religious Educational Association, Inc., 145 Fifth Ave., McKeesport, Pa., June, 1960: "How West Virginia Votes Were Bought." Alleges bribery.

October, 1960, pp. 1–4: "A Call for Prayer Before the Elections," by Jos. Zacchello. Cites the danger facing the U.S. from the rising power of the Church of Rome in this country while it declines in traditionally Catholic countries. Kennedy, if elected, would be subject to enormous clerical pressure along lines of special Catholic interest. He has never said whether or not he would be willing to sign and administer a U.S. law for public aid to birth-control programs.

Pp. 11–12: "For Puzzled Protestants," by William H. Worrilow, Jr. The puzzle is found in Kennedy's statements and positions on policy matters—an ambassador to the Vatican, public funds for nonpublic schools—which seem to be at variance with those of the hierarchy.

Pp. 13–18: "Every Catholic Must Conform," reprinted from *Protestant Action,* August, 1960. A comment on the article *"Punti Fermi"* in the May 18, 1960, issue of *Osservatore Romano.* Because of the sensation it caused in U.S. politics, the entire text as it appeared in *Our Sunday Visitor* is reprinted.

CRISWELL, DR. W. A., see *Religious Freedom, the Church, the State and Senator Kennedy.*

Cut Loose from Rome (pamphlet), by Albert W. Bell, 2236 Madison Ave., Ogden, Utah. Stresses the political power and pretensions of Rome. No man can be a Roman Catholic and an American "Catholic" at the same time.

Danger: A Catholic for U.S.A. President (leaflet), message by Clarence E. Fast, Baptist minister, member of National Association of Evangelicals, Grace Missionary Church, Zion, Ill., Sunday evening, August 21, 1960. America faces one of its greatest threats in this election year. Fast is opposed to Kennedy on church-state grounds as well as on grounds of his "liberal ideology."

A Dangerous Doctrine (28-page pamphlet), sermon by Batsell Barrett Baxter, Hillsboro Church of Christ, 2206 Hillsboro Rd., Nashville, Tenn., October 9, 1960. Calls on every non-Catholic to be vigilant in preventing the Roman Church from gaining further advantage until such time as it changes its policy of intolerance toward other religions. When the Catholic Church solidly controls a country, religious freedom dies. Proof: Catholic persecution of Protestants in Latin American countries, and statements of the Church's doctrine from such sources as the *Syllabus,* Connell, *Civiltà,* and Ryan and Boland.

The Defender (weekly magazine), ed. by Grover Stevens and Ferrell Jenkins, pub. by the Spring and Blaine Church of Christ, 3800 Blaine Ave., St. Louis 10, Mo., October 2, 1960: "How To Identify the One True Church," ninth in a series on Catholicism. In the question period after the Houston speech, Kennedy refused to deny the doctrine of mental reservation.

76

August 4, 1960: "Kennedy Obeys Catholic Church." Author is disturbed over clerical pressure which, allegedly, prevented Kennedy from attending the dedication of a chapel in Philadelphia in 1950.

Destiny: The Magazine of National Life, pub. by Destiny Publishers, Merrimac, Mass., September, 1960: "Why Not a Roman Catholic President?"

A Devout Roman Catholic for President of the U.S.??? (24-page booklet), by Willard H. Pope, pub. by Stonerock Bible Chapel, Inc., Ada, Kan. Opposed to socialism, communism, the U.N., the World Council of Churches, the National Council of the Churches of Christ, and to Kennedy—a Catholic—for President because the hierarchy demands the first allegiance of its subjects.

Dilling Bulletin (mimeographed sheet), ed. by Elizabeth Dilling, Box 659, Chicago 90, Ill., May–June, 1960. Pinpoints the basic danger as that coming from the "Talmudists."

September–October, 1960: "The 1960 Election." Claims that the Catholic Church is not really taking over the world but, like all Christian churches, is falling daily under the Talmudic ax.

Do You Want To See This? (cartoon), dist. by Rose Park Baptist Church, Rev. Garland Cofield, pastor, Holland, Mich. Theme: Pope John wielding a whip over a prostrate Uncle Sam.

Dr. Berry's Newsletter (4-page newspaper), ed. and pub. by Charles A. Berry, Box 1141, Arcadia, Cal., August, 1960, p. 1: "Catholic Power Now Controls National Politics." Warns of Catholic control in civic life.

The Enemy Within Our Borders (tract), comp. by Rev. G. de Champlain, former Roman Catholic priest, pub. by Osterhus Publishing Co., 4500 West Broadway, Minneapolis 22, Minn. The hierarchy is identified as the "enemy," with its aim of capturing the White House and ruling over this great Protestant nation. Catholics take orders from "the man-God in the Vatican."

Evangelical Mennonite (monthly magazine), ed. by Don W. Klopfenstein, official organ of the Conference of Evangelical Mennonites, Grabill, Ind., September 15, 1960: "Catholic President? Religious Freedom, the Church, the State and Senator Kennedy." A reprint of the Criswell sermon.

Exposé—Catholic Plan To Control the U.S. and How To Win the Catholics to Christ (booklet), by Harry Hampel, Evangelist, P.O. Box 8646, Dallas, Tex.

FEDERAL PARTY, Merrill J. Fox, dir., 401 South La Salle St., Chicago 5, Ill. A letter dated Chicago, May, 9, 1960, deplores the denial of church-state separation taught by the Catholics. Quotes from a "Church Resolution" printed in *The Daily Olympian* (Olympia, Wash.), May, 1960: "The American Council of Christian Churches registers its disapproval of a Roman Catholic for President."

THE FINISHED WONDER (32-page tiny booklet), by Ray W. Johnson, ex-priest. Advertises *Fifty Years in the Church of Rome,* by Charles Chiniquy.

First the Ballot Box, then The Cross (4-page leaflet), by Don Hillis, pub. by H. M. Hillis, 600 Fairmont, Glendale 3, Cal. Predicts that a Roman Catholic can become President only if many people put their political party ahead of Christianity, that is, the ballot box ahead of the cross. The reasoning is that the Roman Catholic hierarchy wants to push the Bible out of American education so that the Roman Church can then demand public tax money to support its own parochial schools. Proof: Governor Brown, when attorney general of California, made a ruling against Bible reading in public schools.

Foes of Freedom (2-page mimeo sheet), sermon by Rev. W. S. Stoddard, Presbyterian, July 17, 1960. Expresses grave concern about the Catholic Church with its drive for temporal and political power, its conniving for special privilege, its infiltration of significant government posts, and the proven duplicity of Roman Catholicism in achieving its secular aims.

Free Humanist (magazine), 5526 Westford Rd., Philadelphia 20, Pa., September, 1960: "Who Are the Bigots?" by Martin A.

78

Larson. Warns of the recent drive against "bigotry" by the Catholic hierarchy. Claims that this hierarchy is "working day and night to gain more and more untrammelled power, so that one day it will control American life as once it dominated Europe. So now this insidious enemy in our midst, which we have nurtured as a serpent in our bosom, giving it liberties it would never grant to us, claims more rights, than any others among our citizens enjoy; it demands for itself immunities which even now it proclaims must never be allowed to error— that is, to Protestantism, or to any other ideological deviations" (p. 3).

FRESHWATER, HUGH J., 369 Williams Ave., Salt Lake City 11, Utah. A 4-page letter, "Dear Brothers," calling on all children of Israel to vote against the Roman Catholic candidate for President because if he is elected the children of Jacob and the State of Israel will be discriminated against. The Roman Catholic Church has always sought to destroy the children of Israel.

THE FUNDAMENTALIST (magazine), official voice of the World Baptist Fellowship, Box 125, Jacksonville, Fla., August, 1960: "Christians United for a Free America," by George L. Norris, chmn. An organization set up to oppose the election of Kennedy. Norris claims that the Kennedy backers are probably circulating copies of the bogus K. of C. oath in order to make Kennedy a martyr and thus win sympathy and support, since it is widely known that the oath is a bogus.

"If John F. Kennedy Is Elected . . . Let's Talk About Immediate Results," by Dr. Ray Tatum. Author claims that there would be no immediate loss of liberty, but the establishment of a precedent and the growth of power and prestige. Worst of all, the position of President would be subject to a foreign head of the Roman Catholic Church.

GOOD CITIZENSHIP CAMPAIGN, Scottish Rite, 825 Union Ave., Memphis, Tenn. A 12-page letter urges all Masons to vote. Claims not to be anti-Catholic or anti-Negro but to be pro-Masonic, pro-Protestant, and pro-Jewish. The Pope has urged all Catholics to engage actively in politics, and has stated frankly that the hierarchy and the priesthood have the right and duty to guide them.

Gospel Advocate (weekly), Seventh Ave., Nashville, Tenn., August 11, 1960: "Kennedy Advocated Public Funds for Parochial Schools," by E. Claude Gardner. A bill introduced by Representative Kennedy in 1949 in the 81st Congress, H.R. 5838, is cited as an example of yielding to clerical pressure.

September 22, 1960: "Kennedy Refuses to Deny Doctrine of Mental Reservation on Houston TV Program," by V. E. Howard. In the Houston TV exchange, Kennedy said that if his Church should bring pressure to bear on him which would be in conflict with his American duties as President of the United States, he would resign as President. Mr. Howard notes that Kennedy said he would resign as President, not as a Catholic, which is an open admission that he owes his allegiance first and last to the Pope in Rome.

Gospel Defender (monthly magazine), ed. and pub. by Howard A. Blazer, Sr., 118 North Seminary Rd., Florence, Ala. Articles on "Abraham Lincoln's Prophecy" and "The White House—American or Roman?" by V. E. Howard.

Gospel Hour News, ed. by V. E. Howard, P.O. Box 113, Greenville, Tex., August 31, 1960: "Kennedy's Millions Has the Smell of Whiskey."

April 30, 1960: "What About a Catholic President?"

The Greater Danger (10-page brochure), by Jos. P. Kamp, pub. by Headlines, Box 333 Westport, Conn. Links Kennedy with the social welfare state, socialism, and communism, and this is *the* real danger.

The Greater Nebraskan (monthly newspaper), Omaha, Neb., August, 1960: " 'New Horizons—The Young Deal' and John F. Kennedy," by George J. Thomas. Opposed to Kennedy because of his liberal views, endorsement of big government, free government spending, and softness toward communism. If elected, Kennedy would change the U.S. from a republic

80

to a Socialist nation and thus advance the cause of communism.

Here Are the Facts: Let the Roman Church Speak for Herself (4-page leaflet), by Dr. Harvey H. Springer and Dr. Fred Garland, P.O. Box 90, Englewood, Col. Series of questions and answers condemning Catholicism out of its own mouth.

The Herndon News (periodical), August 31, 1960: "Oppose Roman Catholic President," by Thomas E. Baker, pastor, Paxton Bible Church, Herndon, Pa. Says that, according to the teachings of his Church, a Roman Catholic cannot honestly take the oath of office of the President of the U.S. and remain a true Catholic. But a Catholic official does not have to be honest when taking the oath of office—he may employ the practice of mental reservation.

Home Rule, Not Rome Rule (handbill). The brothers Kennedy are Romans (Political) with first allegiance to a foreign state, the Vatican. America is the most tolerant of all nations to religious beliefs, but no Roman Political can be our President.

Hoodwinking Protestants (16-page pamphlet), by L. H. Lehmann, pub. as Christian Heritage Pamphlet, Series P, by Christ's Mission, Box 925, Sea Cliff, L.I., N.Y. Claims that the Knights of Columbus Information Bureau is trying to play down the official teaching of the Church and make it appear harmless to Protestants in order to lull them into believing that Catholic teaching does not differ much from that of Protestants on such matters as sin, salvation, marriage, education, separation of church and state, public schools, and the like. But the truth is that Catholics want religious freedom only for themselves; they oppose public schools and the separation of church and state.

How the Roman Catholic Church Would Change the Constitution (1-page sheet), reprinted from *Church and State* (*q.v.*), May, 1960. A presentation, drawn from *Catholic Lawyer*, Winter, 1960, of "the Catholic Position" regarding the meaning of the First Amendment as contrasted with the Supreme Court's position as explicated in *Everson* and *McCollum*. The point is to show that Catholics use the words *church, state,* and *separation* in a distorted way and do not adhere to the Supreme Court's interpretation.

How Would You Answer Kennedy's Loaded Question? (tract), by Joel Darby, pub. by Osterhus Publishing Co., 4500 West Broadway, Minneapolis 22, Minn. The question is the one asked by Kennedy at the Houston talk: "Did forty million American Catholics lose their chance of being President on the day they were baptized?" Darby suggests the following way of reply: "Jesus would answer: 'Whose inscription is on the textbooks these millions of baptized Catholic children must study?' The Pope's!"

Human Events, 408 First St., S.E., Washington 3, D.C., June 2, 1960: "Kennedy for President? A Catholic Priest Says 'No.' " by Rev. J. B. Carol. An attack upon liberalism, Kennedy's political and economic philosophy, originally given as a speech to a Catholic audience. Printed in *Human Events* with the omission of three key paragraphs which applied the condemnation of "liberalism" equally to so-called "Modern Republicanism." Kennedy supporters objected to this editing device, and *Human Events* later published an account of the controversy which included the omitted paragraphs: "Father Carol's 'Kennedy for President? No!'—The Story of the Campaign's No. 1 Document" (December 1, 1960).

I Was a Roman Priest (4-page leaflet), by Rev. John Zanon, pub. by Pilgrim Tract Society, Inc., Randleman, N.C. Author says that reading the Bible convinced him of the error of Roman Catholicism.

If America Elects a Catholic President (6-page leaflet), by Don Hillis, Glendale 3, Cal. Predicts the end of 101 liberties which are enjoyed only in Protestant countries if America elects a Catholic President. Rome does not really accept church-state separation except for expediency. Roman Catholicism has steadily been gaining power in the U.S., so that now it intimidates Congress, censors and silences the opposition, collects vast sums from the public treasury, and drives toward official recognition and establishment.

If the U.S. Becomes 51% Catholic! (leaflet), by C. Stanley Lowell, reprinted from *Christianity Today*, dist. by POAU, 1633 Massachusetts Ave., N.W., Washington 6, D.C. A sophisticated, though distorted, presentation drawn from Catholic sources of the dangers to religious liberty if Catholicism gains a majority status.

If You Love the American Way of Life, Believe in Freedom of Religion and Democracy, You Should Read This Article (5 mimeographed pages), by W. J. Newell, 2745 Ludelle St., Fort Worth, Tex. Points to the history of the combination of church and state which always leads to totalitarian government. Thinks Kennedy should appeal to the Pope to renounce his right in political matters and to state clearly that he (the Pope) believes in the democratic way of life and the right of freedom of worship. The Church should renounce all "cordates" (evidently concordats) now in force so that there might be religious freedom.

If You Vote for a Catholic for President or Vice-President, America Will Be Under a Dictatorship—the Pope! (pamphlet), pub. by Kane Ministry, Inc., 217 Woodland Ave., Merchantville, N.J.

If You Want the Pope for President Vote a Catholic into the White House (tract), by R. Frazier, pub. by Osterhus Publishing Co., 4500 West Broadway, Minneapolis 22, Minn. A compilation of quotations from authoritative Catholic statements, or from writings approved by the Roman Catholic Church.

Internationaletter (monthly newsletter), comp. by the Public Relations Department of the International Council of Christian Churches, 801 Haddon Ave., Collingswood, N.J., September, 1960. Contains a condemnation of the Democratic National Committee's Office of Community Relations because of its memorandum naming two officials of the American and International Councils of Christian Churches as "promoters of religious hatred." The memorandum was prepared by James Wine, Presbyterian elder, who resigned his position with the National Council of the Churches of Christ in order to serve as religious affairs advisor to Kennedy during the campaign. Rev. Harvey Springer, ACCC and ICCC executive committee member, and Rev. Carl McIntire, ICC president, were the two named by the Democratic National Committee memo.

Is It "Religion" or a Trojan Horse? (brochure), by Luther A. Smith, reprinted from *The New Age* (see *Catholicism—Religion . . .*), October, 1960. Claims that it is not the Roman Catholic manner of worship which causes apprehension but the historic record of Roman Catholic clericalism with its centuries-long grasping for material wealth and political power.

Is Religion Only a Campaign Issue? (11-page booklet), by Rev. Paul P. Fryhling, senior minister, First Covenant Church, Minneapolis, Minn., pub. by Book and Tract Committee, 810 South Seventh St., Minneapolis, Minn. Claims that a candidate is unqualified for high executive office if his religion limits him in the discharge of the duties and the spirit of the Constitution and the laws of the land. This would be the case with one who owes a supreme, ultimate obedience to a hierarchy of men outside the United States.

Is a Roman Catholic Qualified for Public Office? (1-page sheet), Citizens Committee, P.O. Box 137, Limerick, Pa. Devoted to "America's Questions and Roman Catholic Answers," called "Bulletin of Roman Catholic Quotations." For example: "Does the Catholic Church actually oppose our system of Democracy and American way of life?" The Catholic answer: ". . . institution diametrically opposed to our doctrine, namely, Capitalism as it is carried on in the world and especially in the U.S." The allegedly "Catholic" answer is obviously very confusing, as it is excerpted from the article "Communism: A Reply," by Bertrand Weaver, C.P., *Catholic World*, January, 1938, p. 400, addressed to the article "How Not To Fight Communism," by S. J. Rueve, S.J., *Catholic World*, November, 1937, pp. 138–143. Father Rueve was simply indicating some of the difficulties and shortcomings of an "anti-communism" based solely on textbook syllogisms and divorced from the existential reality of communism, which is the political-social-religious system of life actually at work in the Soviet Union.

Israeli Press Views Nixon and Kennedy (brochure), reprinted from *The Jerusalem Post Weekly* (Tel Aviv), and *Which of the Two Is Better for Jesus?* (brochure), by Isaac Remba, reprinted from *Heruth* (Tel Aviv daily, organ of the National Liberal Party), September 9, 1960, pub. by Committee for Human Rights, 100 East 42nd St., New York 17, N.Y.

An Issue To Be Faced (9-page mimeographed pamphlet), sermon by Rev. Henry C. Beatty, pastor, First Methodist Church, Gering, Neb. Expresses a sincere concern about the compatibility of Catholic church-state doctrine with the American Protestant-inspired concept of religious freedom. Notes the tendency of the Church to dictate to political leaders in such countries as Argentina, Spain, Paraguay. Proposes basic questions to be put to both candidates:

"1. What is your attitude toward the plan of financing parochial schools with public funds by scholarship grants to parents of children in such schools at the elementary and secondary levels?

"2. Pope Pius IX, in the Syllabus of Errors, condemned the concept of the separation of church and state. Do you accept the position of the Roman Catholic Church or the American principle of the separation of church and state as provided for in the Constitution?

"3. Many nations recognize the Vatican City as both church and state and send official ambassadors to the Holy See. If you become President, what would be your policy concerning the appointment of an ambassador from the United States or a personal representative to the Vatican?

"4. As our chief executive, would you support the use of public funds for the dissemination of birth control information and material when requested by other nations facing over-population? Would you continue to support the granting of federal funds to hospitals in the U.S. which disseminate birth control information?"

The Issue Before Us (6-page pamphlet), by Harold E. Lindsey, First Baptist Church, Waco, Tex., July 27, 1960, dist. by Scottish Rite Masons, Portland, Ore. Author notes four reasons why Kennedy must not be elected, for the ultimate danger is that we will be subject to the power of Rome:

1. As a Roman Catholic, Kennedy would be subject to the traditional pressures which have characterized the Catholic Church's bid for power for centuries. These pressures result from the theological conviction that the Church is supreme over the state and should control the state. The Roman Church's doctrine on church and state has not changed, nor has its design to control nations in a practical way.
2. He would be subject to a power other than God, his conscience, or his country.
3. The Catholic Church would project itself into the affairs of state through him.
4. He could not carry out his duties as President and remain in good standing with his Church.

What to expect if Mr. Kennedy is elected:

1. The first amendment will be jeopardized in insidious ways.
2. Federal money will begin to flow to Catholic institutions.
3. There will be changes in the fields of medicine, censorship, and domestic relations.

The Issue of a Catholic President (folder), by J. Sidney Sample. This folder was put in Baptist Church bulletins in Columbia, S.C., and elsewhere. Aim: to inform voters, not to tell them how to vote. They need to know what the Roman Catholic Church is and what John F. Kennedy is. The Church is a dictator to its subjects, and endeavors to combine church and state. Evidence for this opinion is drawn from *Mirari Vos;* John McKay; the May 18, 1960, issue of *Osservatore Romano; Christianity Today;* and *Church and State* (POAU).

John Kennedy is an avowed Catholic. He will kneel to the Pope although for the moment he is allowed some independence in speaking, probably as a tactic of the larger Vatican strategy.

The Issue of a Roman Catholic President (3 mimeographed pages), by W. O. Vaught, Jr., pastor, Immanuel Baptist Church, Little Rock, Ark. A trip through Central and South America showed the author the results of Catholic power and pressure, which have so disadvantaged Protestant missionaries. Now the bid is for control of the U.S. The most powerful lobby in Washington is that of the Roman Catholic Church. Over 90 percent of the millions of dollars released to hospitals by the Hill-Burton Act has gone to Catholic institutions. Kennedy will undoubtedly be subject to and influenced by clerical pressure.

It Happened This Way (booklet), by Ray W. Johnson, pub. by The Life Messengers, Box 1967, Seattle 11, Wash. Purports to be the true story of the Roman Catholic Church.

Jewish "Manifesto" Proclamation of 1860 (1-page flier, printed on 2 sides), pub. by Keep America Committee, P.O. Box 3094, Los Angeles 54, Cal., Ned Harman, exec. Sec'y., P.O. Box 441, Wetumpka, Ala. Addressed to the Jews of the world. Anti-Jewish and anti-Catholic in tone. If you are a Christian, patriotic American, you almost have to be anti-Semitic.

KENNEDY IS NOT FIT TO BE PRESIDENT, *The Pink Punk Pro-Red Record of Senator Kennedy,* and *The True Inside Story of the Rigging and Fixing at the Democratic Convention in Los Angeles* (3 pamphlets), by Dan Gilbert, Upland, Cal. The author, an active anti-Catholic pamphleteer, attacks Senator Kennedy in these three reports, questioning his patriotism and fitness to be President because of his religious affiliation.

Kennedy Supports Pope's Orders of Segregation by Creed (flier), by O. C. Miller, copy of a weekly column which goes to about fifty religious publications in the U.S., dist. by Capital Writers Bureau, Wash., D.C. Claims that Kennedy lends his support to this narrowness in the churches and the schools.

KNIGHTS OF COLUMBUS OATH. Various bogus versions of the oath were widely circulated throughout the country, and were apparently designed to breed hatred and intolerance, regardless of truth. In answer, the Knights of Columbus published *Criminal Libels Against the Knights of Columbus Exposed,* New Haven, Conn., 1960.

Let Freedom Ring (31-page pamphlet), pub. by Bible Correspondence School, 6840 Eastern Ave., N.W., Washington 12, D.C. Objects to the "teaching" of the Catholic Church about the union of church and state.

Let's Face the Issue (4-page leaflet), by William Van Orden, pub. by *Herald of Truth,* Box 57, Kingsville, Md. Warns against Kennedy's "brainwash" statement made before the Greater Houston Ministerial Association. Claims that the Church is of necessity intolerant and only endures heresy when she must. If Catholics ever gain an immense numerical majority, it will mean the end of religious freedom in this country.

The Liberal, Bulletin of Friendship (a rationalist and free-thought monthly journal), pub. by Liberal League, Inc., 5233 North Fifth St., Philadelphia 20, Pa., September, 1960, pp. 11–12: "Catholicism and the Presidency," by Luther A. Smith. Claims that the canon law of the Roman Church and the directives of the Pope validate the fears of the people that the dual allegiance of American Catholics is a present danger to our free institutions.

Pp. 13–16: "The Vatican Over the White House," by Martin A. Larson. Sees as the only real issue in the campaign the decision of the American people as to whether they will place a subject of the Pope, a foreign prelate, with his monstrous claim to infallibility, in the White House. Predicts dire things for the U.S. if a Catholic is elected President. The program of a Catholic administration would include: (1) violations of the first amendment, (2) reversal of the McCollum and Everson cases, (3) censorship, (4) outlawing of birth-control information, (5) prohibition of divorce, (6) outlawing of mixed marriages, (7) monopoly of decent government jobs by Catholics, (8) increase in tax-free enterprises owned and operated by the hierarchy, (9) decline of public secular universities, and (10) public subsidies for large families. Preliminary preparation for this program would include: (1) establishment of a Fascist-theocratic state, (2) hounding humanists, rationalists, masons, and secularists out of society or reducing them to abject silence, and (3) persecuting Protestants as "heretics." Ultimately, there would be an end to freedom of thought in science, politics, religion, philosophy, and economics, and the U.S. would retrogress into barbarism.

October, 1960, pp. 10–11: "Religious Issue in the Presidential Campaign," by Dr. Oscar Riddle, pres., American Rationalist Federation. Finds the Catholic opposition to birth control to be the precise point of entrance of the religious issue. Hinders our foreign aid program.

Lincoln's Assassins (29-page booklet), by Justin D. Fulton, D.D., pub. by Christ's Mission, 369 Carpenter Ave., Sea Cliff, L.I., N.Y., 1958. Links Church of Rome with the assassination of Lincoln. Because this Church is still in our midst, fearful responsibilities devolve upon the American people.

The Lutheran Witness (weekly magazine), September 20, 1960): "We Believe, Teach and Confess: Church and State," by Carl A. Eberhard. The article contrasts the Lutheran position on church-state separation with the Catholic. Source for the former: *The Blood of Concord,* Muhlenberg Press, 1959; for the latter: *Unam sanctam* of Boniface VIII and the May 18, 1960, article in *Osservatore Romano.*

Pp. 5–6, 19: "Is There a Religious Issue in the Presidential Campaign?" Deplores the slanderous attacks on the presidential nominee because of his religious beliefs. Nevertheless, expresses sincere concern about the danger of Roman domination, the lack of freedom of a Catholic in making political decisions: "The one question Americans have the constitutional right to ask, the one question that must be answered if the religious issue is to be eliminated from the campaign, as it should be, is this: 'Will Senator Kennedy be permitted to follow his own course in supporting public education and complete separation of church and state, or will the Roman Catholic Church, which officially opposes church-state separation, bring the weight of papal pressure to bear on his conscience?' " (p. 6). Wants the Roman Catholic Church to speak out in approval of Senator Kennedy's pledge to uphold the Constitution of the United States.

McBirnie News Letter: The News in the Light of the Bible, ed. by William S. McBirnie, Sr., and Howard Estep, pub. by McBirnie's, Inc., P.O. Drawer 470, Colton, Cal., October, 1960: "U.S.A. at Crossroads: A Roman Catholic President??" Insists that the main reason the Protestants are up in arms against a Roman Catholic for President is the question of subservience to the Pope of Rome, a foreigner and ruler of another state.

MAKE THE WORLD OURS and *Do You Know About Roman Catholic Aspirations?* (2 tracts), pub. by Osterhus Publishing Co., 4500 West Broadway, Minneapolis 22, Minn. Quotes taken from a letter allegedly written by Father Patrick Henry O'Brien to Rev. A. Di Domenica, a former Catholic, of Philadelphia, Pa.

Many Faiths—One Freedom (pamphlet), address by Dick Houston Hall, Jr., at the Eleventh National Conference on Church and State, St. Louis, Mo., 1959, pub. by Protestants and Other Americans United, 1633 Massachusetts Ave., N.W., Washington 6, D.C. Of the 258 denominations in America, only one persistently seeks the support of the government, in violation of church-state separation. Thus, totalitarian domination of our country seems to be the logical purpose of the Roman Catholic Church.

Masonic Home Journal (8-page newspaper), official organ of the Grand Lodge of Kentucky, October 1, 1960, pp. 1, 4: "Grand Master's Message," by John R. Vinson, Jr. Points to the incompatibility of Catholic and American views of church-state separation.

Masonic Inspiration, Free and Independent Masonic News Bulletin, pub. by Charles Van Cott, 32°, Morris Plains, N.J., September, 1960: "Catholic President Question Arouses All America." The move to elect a Catholic President has been a Romanist scheme for centuries. The Vatican plans far ahead, and even though its religio-political empire has fallen in the past, it always bounces back.

October, 1960: "City Hall," by Edward O'Neill. Account of a 1957 meeting of New York politicos (many of them Catholics) who fashioned the plan for capturing the big-city political organizations for Kennedy in 1960.

Members of Congress (Senate and House), Fellow Americans, Sisters and Brothers in God's Spiritual Family on Earth (1-page typed memorandum), by David Darrin, 140 Constitution Ave., N.E., Washington, D.C. Alerts readers to danger of political fascism. Nixon, too, is alleged to be secretly a Catholic and married to a Catholic. Thus, both Kennedy and Nixon must be knocked off in the primaries or at the conventions to thwart this typical Roman Catholic political trickery.

Memorandum (8-page leaflet), pub. by the Democratic National Committee, 1001 Connecticut Ave., N.W., Washington 6, D.C. Answers by Kennedy to questions on church-state issues: separation of church and state; an ambassador to the Vatican; aid to parochial schools; birth control; the Poling incident; the position of the Roman Catholic Church on the First Amendment; the Knights of Columbus oath; oath of office taken by members of Congress.

The Menace (4-page leaflet), by Syd Youngsma, pub. by Faith, Prayer and Tract League, Grand Rapids, Mich. Concerned about the energy, power, and drive of Catholic pressure as it seeks to dominate the U.S. The totalitarian hierarchy of the Catholic Church is incompatible with American democracy.

The Menace of Roman Catholicism (23-page tract), by Earl West, pub. by Religious Book Service, 722 North Payton Rd., Indianapolis 19, Ind. Claims that Roman Catholicism is a bar-

91

rier to every democratic principle of life and is a kind of Trojan horse which has entered America as a threat to our democracy.

A Message to Catholics: Can Devout Catholics Be Loyal Americans? (tract), by Emmett McLoughlin, former Franciscan priest, pub. by Osterhus Publishing Co., 4500 West Broadway, Minneapolis 22, Minn. Admits that the general run of devout Catholics believe that there is no conflict between Americanism and Catholicism because the hierarchy keeps them in ignorance. But, the author insists, "an intelligent, loyal American cannot be a sincere, devout Catholic."

The Methodist Challenge (monthly magazine reaching nearly 18,000 ministers and laymen in every state), 1801 South Flower St., Los Angeles 15, Cal., July, 1960: "Religion and Our Country," by Robert P. Shuler, ed. Asks loyal Protestant Americans to pause and consider the historic facts, which support the conclusion that no man can be wholly loyal to the Catholic Church and to the United States at the same time because of basic points of disagreement between them.

My Life in the Convent (tract), by Margaret Shepherd, pub. by Book and Bible House, Rev. Fred Junior, pubr., Box 3598 University Sta., Gainesville, Fla. (Rev. Junior is the successor to Rev. L. J. King, converted Catholic.)

My Reservations About Voting for a Roman Catholic for U.S. President (leaflet), by Roy Pearson, dean, Andover Newton Theological School, reprinted from *United Church Herald*, February 4, 1960. Dean Pearson's reservations stem from what he thinks is an inevitable subjection of the individual conscience (of the Catholic) to ecclesiastical authority. He fears the danger that the liberal elements within American Catholicism will be swallowed up in centuries of dogma and tradition. Thus, they may begin to take seriously certain official pronouncements of their faith that they have previously disregarded in favor of the good of the nation.

Nashville Tennessean, August 15, 1960, pp. 1–2: "Ministers See

Pulpit Attacks on Kennedy Bid," by James Talley. Reports that many Southern Baptist preachers and Church of Christ ministers would ask their congregations to vote against Senator Kennedy, a Catholic. Thus, Dr. Ramsey Pollard, pastor of Bellevue Baptist Church, Memphis, and president of the Southern Baptist Convention, predicted that an overwhelming majority of the more than 31,000 Baptist preachers in the South would take to their pulpits to oppose Kennedy. Dr. Carroll B. Ellis, a prominent minister in the Church of Christ, said that most of the ministers of that denomination would devote one or more sermons to explaining why the members of their congregations should not vote for a Catholic.

NEWLY, J. EDWIN, 1137 South Calumet St., Kokomo, Ind. A letter, "Dear Friend," warns that all those interested in the continuation of freedom should beware of both Catholics and Communists. The latter want freedom for their ideology only; the former want freedom for their church only. Catholics think that Potestants are heretics who, if they cannot be converted by peaceful means, should be tormented into submission or killed.

NEWMAN, E. P. S., Central Bldg., Washington 4, D.C. A 2-page letter, "Fellow Americans," concerning the presidential election of 1960. In spite of Kennedy's statement at Houston that he would make political decisions according to what his conscience told him was in the national interest, Newman warns that this conscience was formed within the Catholic tradition which accepts the infallibility of the Pope.

The News (8-page leaflet), pub. Curwensville, Pa. Foresees that Kennedy, as the first Catholic President, will support separation of church and state. But the door will be opened for another Catholic later, who will send an ambassador to the Vatican, give state support to parochial schools, and finally, recognize the Catholic Church above all America. Thus, religious liberty will die in this country as it has died in Spain,

Colombia, and wherever the Roman Catholic hierarchy has power to destroy it. The Protestant contention is not for mere toleration but for absolute liberty.

No Freedom of Religion (8-page mimeographed pamphlet), anonymous. Says that a Catholic President would be bound to follow tenets which conflict with American democratic principles.

The Origins and Claims of Roman Catholicism (35-page booklet), by Roy E. Cogdill, Box 980, Lufkin, Tex. The purpose of the study is to "affirm that Catholicism originated in apostasy, that it is not just a religious institution but is political as well, that its cardinal claims are false and its aims both un-Christian and un-American" (p. 3). For example, Catholics believe in the union of church and state, oppose the free public school system, and aim to bring America under the dictatorship of the Pope.

The Patriot Press, October 24, 1960: "The Truth About Bigotry" (also published as a 4-page flier). Asserts that Roman Catholicism dictates to its members how they shall vote and where and when they shall enjoy free speech. The real enemy is Roman Catholic political power and financial greed. Kennedy is a proved bigot because at the order of the Cardinal of Philadelphia, he canceled a speech he was to give at a banquet honoring the four patriotic chaplains who died when the *Dorchester* sank.

Pentecostal Free-Will Baptist Messenger, ed. by Rev. Herbert Carter, P.O. Box 505, Clinton, N.C., August, 1960, pp. 2, 10: "Should We Elect a Roman Catholic President?" Says that the 1948 bishops' statement denounced separation of church and state as the "shibboleth of doctrinaire secularism." Catholics were summoned to work for its destruction.

A Plea for American Fair Play (4 mimeographed pages), radio message by Rev. Baxton Bryant, minister, Elmwood Methodist Church, 1315 Berkley, Dallas, Tex., given over Station KIXL, sponsored by the Young Democrats of Dallas County in answer to the Criswell sermon of July 3, 1960. Bryant insists that in this time of crisis, we cannot afford to mark off 40,000,000 Americans as unfit for office on account of religious prejudice. The real issue in the campaign is leadership, not religion. Those who are overly concerned about the latter do not understand the system of checks and balances written into the Constitution. For example, all major appointments must be confirmed by an overwhelmingly Protestant Senate. All actions may ultimately have to face the test of constitutionality according to the judgment of a Protestant Supreme Court.

The Pope for President (leaflet), by Joseph Zacchello, pub. by *The Convert* (*q.v.*). The target of this attack is the Roman Catholic hierarchy and its power over laymen. "To vote for a Roman Catholic, just because he is a Roman Catholic, is like voting the Pope into the White House. . . ."

The Pope's Intention in America: A Fateful Situation Revealed (6-page tract), by E. C. Fuqua, pub. by *The Vindicator* (*q.v.*). Warns that Roman Catholicism is America's number one enemy. Cited in proof is the bishop's oath, according to the testimony of a certain Patrick O'Brien of Rochester, N.Y.: "We, the Hierarchy of the Holy Roman Catholic Church, expect all loyal children of the Church to assist the President with all our strength to see that individuals comprising the U.S. Supreme Court shall obey the President's injunction, and if necessary we shall change, amend, or blot out the present Constitution so that the President may enforce his, or rather our, humanitarian program and all phases of human rights as laid down by our saintly Popes and the Holy Mother Church" (p. 2).

A Presbyterian Looks at the Presidency (leaflet), sermon by Rev. Roy T. Sherrod, minister, First Presbyterian Church, Waco, Tex., September 11, 1960. A measured consideration of some legitimate questions, for example, (1) church and state in Catholic doctrine compared with what Tillich calls the Protestant principle—"God and conscience over State and Church"; (2) how American or how Roman is the Roman Catholic candidate for the presidency? Quotes from the 1960 minutes of the General Assembly of the Presbyterian Church, U.S.: "(1) That the General Assembly does not deem it appropriate to its function to endorse or condemn any individual candidate for public office; (2) That we do not have a clear and consistent statement from the Roman Catholic Church concerning the freedom of the individual member's conscience in dealing with matters of public policy; and (3) That such an expression as the resolution calls for would be misunderstood as religious prejudice or bigotry. Further, that reaffirming the historic American position with respect to the separation of Church and State, we encourage all Presbyterians to exercise their responsible role as citizens to determine the basic issues in any campaign, recognizing that the candidates' personal faith in God, their integrity and their positions concerning public policy are more important than their denominational or party affiliation" (p. 6).

Pronouncements of the Roman Catholic Church, by Salem V. Smith, 226 State St., New London, Conn. A series of quotes taken out of context which convey an erroneous impression.

Prophecies for the Times, No. 8 (96-page booklet), pub. by G. E. Lowman, St. Petersburg 33, Fla. On the question of whether or not a Roman Catholic should be President of the United States, the issue is clear. Such a man would have to say "yes" to Rome or "no" to Rome. In the latter case, he would incur anathema from the Pope according to the teaching of Catholicism. Thus, to be true to the teachings of his church, a Roman Catholic President would have to allow the office of President to be interfered with.

The Prophetic Ensign (24-page magazine), ed. and pub. by Arthur E. Bloomfield, 14 Laurel Oak Drive, Eustis, Fla., September, 1960: "Doctrines that Hide Truth," by A. E. Bloomfield. Asserts that from the prophetic point of view, Romanism is a greater threat to a free world than communism. It gives orders to public officials as to the performance of their patriotic duties.

Protestant Journal (quarterly magazine), July, 1960, p. 6: "Editorial," by Harry Hampel. Cites as reason for opposition to any Catholic politician the fact that the "Roman Catholic hierarchy and the Vatican stand before the world as a secular, political state, ruled as a dictatorship by a secular ruler, an Italian politician—the Pope."

Protestant Union Officials of AFL-CIO or Protestant Rank and File Unionists (Western Union press message), from the Conference of Protestant Workers for Determining Political Strategy, courtesy of Protestant Union Officials of AFL-CIO, 816 Sixteenth St., N.W., Washington, D.C. The message was prefaced by this warning: "Beware Vaticanism. Beware, Take Care of International Catholicism—TRUST HER NOT, she gives a shy glance and looks down, BUT SHE IS FOOLING THEE." The message expresses opposition to Kennedy because of his close ties with Vaticanism (that is, "religious colonialism"), with its worldwide political ambitions. A good Catholic has been brainwashed and disciplined from childhood. His textbooks and his press have been censored. He is subconsciously indoctrinated to an authoritarian dictatorship and despotism.

Protestants, Attention (folder), pub. by the Georgia Bible Institute, Athens, Ga. An appeal to Protestants to help the poor priest-ridden millions of Roman Catholics in the United States.

Protestants, Catholics and Politics (pamphlet), by C. Stanley Lowell, reprinted from *Christianity Today*, pub. by Protestants and Other Americans United, 1633 Massachusetts Ave., N.W., Washington 6, D.C. Lowell claims that there would be intolerable pressures on a Catholic President to support "Catholic" interests, especially federal aid to parochial schools. He says that the whole weight of Catholic action has been thrown into the struggle to change our traditional church-state pattern in favor of an arrangement which would bring a billion and a half dollars in tax funds to the Roman Church annually in the form of education subsidies.

Protestants in a Spiritual Stupor Breed Strong Roman Catholicism (leaflet), by Joseph Zacchello, pub. by *The Convert*

97

(*q.v.*). The nature of the Roman Church has not changed since the horrible crimes of the Dark Ages. The author laments the fact that many Protestants cannot see any danger in having a Catholic as President, and yet their liberties are definitely at stake. More and more Catholics are becoming governors, Senators, Congressmen, servicemen, teachers, journalists, F.B.I. men, and so on. With a Catholic President, the combination would be unbreakable.

PUBLIC SCHOOLS VS. PAROCHIAL SCHOOLS and *Little Known Facts About the Society of Jesus (Jesuits)* (2 mimeographed pieces), by Jack Odom, Box 833, Fort Bragg, Cal.

The Radio Bible Hour: Big John and Little John (1 mimeographed sheet); by J. Harold Smith, Southern Baptist minister, Box 13033, Dallas 20, Tex. Opposed to a Roman Catholic as President because such a man is a member of an "ecclesiastical system" which is so dogmatic and totalitarian that it demands and gets the first allegiance of every one of its members.

The Ramparts We Watch (brochure), address by Glenn Archer at the Southern Baptist Convention, Chicago, Ill., pub. by Protestants and Other Americans United, 1633 Massachusetts Ave., N.W., Washington 6, D.C. The five ramparts watched by POAU are (1) the public school, the basis and bulwark of American democracy; (2) the legal right to existence of parochial schools, at private expense, as a mission of the Church; (3) the First Amendment, the guarantee of the free church and the free pulpit; (4) the legal concept of church-state separation, the only safeguard of religious peace; and (5) free conscience, the key to unlock spiritual power.

RELIGION, A GIGANTIC FRAUD, *Religious Brain Stuffing,* and *The Roman Catholic Church Is a Menace to American Liberty* three 4-page leaflets), by James Harvey Johnson, pub. by Superior Books, Department CC, Box 2832, San Diego 12, Cal. The last-named pamphlet asserts that the Catholic Church is an absolute dictatorship, opposed to all liberties, which plans to make America Catholic.

Religion an Issue in 1960 Presidential Elections? (1-page statement), by Jose M. Garcia, 90 County Rd., Tenafly, N.J. The author, born in Spain a Roman Catholic, came to the U.S. as a nonsectarian. His criticism of the Roman Church centers in the fact that it is a sovereign power, a political state as well as a religion; is not tolerant of other faiths; and denies the validity of church-state separation.

Religion, Politics and the Presidency (leaflet), sermon by Harold J. Ockenga, Park St. Church, Boston, Mass., June 5, 1960. Ockenga warns that we are moving toward an era of Roman Catholic domination in America, and this raises the problem of the incompatibility of Catholic teaching on church and state with the American system. To solve the problem, Rome need only repudiate the view of the *Syllabus of Errors* and *Immortale Dei,* for the statements of some American Catholic spokesmen do not conform to this "official" teaching.

Religion and the Presidency (leaflet), sermon by Robert P. Gates, First Presbyterian Church, Peoria, Ill., March 13, 1960. Believes that it is wrong for any responsible political party to sponsor a Roman Catholic for the presidency because of the fact that the U.S. Constitution was written against a background of Protestant theology. Thus, the religious doctrine of separation of church and state is a Protestant credal belief, and unacceptable to Roman Catholics.

Religious Freedom, the Church, the State and Senator Kennedy (4-page leaflet), sermon by Dr. W. A. Criswell, First Baptist Church, Dallas, Tex., July 3, 1960, pub. by Doniger & Raughley, Inc., Great Neck, L.I., N.Y. The sermon was also noted in the press (one source: the newspaper *Baptist Witness,* ed. by Bradley Lasserre, Jr., pub. by the Baptist Hour, 13 East Mitchell Ave., Cincinnati 17, Ohio, September, 1960). The sermon expresses strong opposition to a Catholic candidate. Criswell's attack centers on the charge that Roman Catholicism is inimical to religious liberty. Religion is a personal, individual, voluntary, and spiritual relationship between a man and his Creator; but "The Roman Catholic institutional

99

hierarchy is not only a religion, it is a political tyranny." Furthermore, its nuns and priests are on public payrolls, but they pay no income tax. An article in the May 18, 1960, issue of *Osservatore Romano* claimed the right of the Church to intervene in the political field to enlighten the consciences of its members.

Because the Doniger & Raughley pamphlet was mailed anonymously, the Senate Subcommittee on Privileges and Elections began an investigation on October 17, 1960, since Federal law forbids anonymous mailing of campaign literature.

The Religious Issue (brochure), pub. by Citizens for Religious Freedom, organized at a conference in Washington, D.C., in September, 1960. Brochure contains ten points against Catholicism:

1. Roman Catholicism is not only a religion to which many of our good friends belong; it is a political force in our society as well.
2. Roman Catholic doctrine and policy are ultimately incompatible with the principle of separation of church and state, the foundation of our freedoms.
3. Wherever Roman Catholicism is the religion of the majority, it attempts to suppress all other religious faiths, and uses secular governments and institutions as a means to impose its system upon the public.
4. The hierarchy insist on controlling laymen in civic and political affairs.
5. The candidate himself has admitted, in effect, that his Church does exert pressure on men in public affairs.
6. The candidate's promise that ecclesiastical pressures would not influence his conduct of the presidency, sincere as it may be, does not prove conclusively that he could fully resist such pressure.
7. The threat of excommunication is used by the hierarchy to enforce its demands on individual members.

8. Some Catholic public officials have used their offices to procure advantages for their Church.

9. There is no evidence that the Roman Catholic hierarchy in the U.S. has any intention of changing its announced objective of procuring public funds and other special benefits for its schools, hospitals, businesses, and other institutions.

10. American citizens must decide individually, knowing the political power of the Roman Catholic hierarchy in the U.S., whether it is wise to elect a President who gives his allegiance to that system.

The "Religious Issue," 1960 (leaflet), sermon by Gaye L. McGlothlen, pastor, Immanuel Baptist Church, Nashville, Tenn., September 11, 1960. Lists the threats to religious freedom which will continue to exist in this country until a Pope, not a bishop or a Catholic layman, says: "Our policy in the U.S. will be different; we will not strive for union of church and state there; we will cease political pressure for tax funds for our schools; and we will stop receiving those political favors now granted to us." Notes ten areas where Vatican policies and hierarchical clericalism pose threats to American freedom:

1. The long-range Catholic plan for America has four parts:
   a. Increase the Catholic population.
   b. Expand Catholic schools with public tax funds.
   c. Capture as many public schools as possible.
   d. Infiltrate as many non-Catholic organizations as possible with Catholic laymen through Catholic action.

2. The long-range Catholic plan for the world will eventuate in a totalitarianism of church control over all elements in nations.

3. The mixed marriage policy of the Church requires that the children be raised as Catholics.

4. Birth control is forbidden.

5. Censorship and boycotts are made use of.

101

6. Public schools are boycotted by Catholics.

7. Increasing demands are made by Catholics for support of parochial schools from the public treasury.

8. The ultimate Catholic goal is union of church and state.

9. There is Catholic insistence that the Constitution be changed.

10. The oath of office is taken with a mental reservation.

The Religious Issue: A Roman Catholic as President (flier), by Robert L. McDonald, Box 724, Lufkin, Tex. The objection is that the Catholic Church claims the power to control civil governments and direct the spiritual affairs of a state.

Reprints from the Baptist Examiner (4-page newspaper format), reprinted "in the interest of religious freedom and the separation of church and state," Ashland, Ky., October, 1960, p. 1: column titled "Hail Mary," by John R. Gilpin. Asserts that Americans would have to hide their faces in shame if a Catholic were elected President, since this would mean a serious inroad into U.S. politics and a step toward the complete domination of America by Roman Catholicism. This is not a matter of politics but of freedom and religious liberty. Says Gilpin: "I would consider myself a traitor to the fifty million Baptists who have been killed by various means of torture at the hands of Roman Catholics if I failed to lift my voice and pen against Mr. Kennedy."

P. 4: "Why I Would Not Vote for a Roman Catholic Candidate," by Bob L. Ross. Except when defined as it wishes, Roman Catholicism opposes the two great landmarks in Baptist history: (1) absolute religious liberty for all, and (2) separation of church and state.

Revival Time's Election Bulletin, by C. M. Ward, pub. by the General Council of the Assemblies of God, Box 70, Springfield, Mo. The issue in the election is that the Catholic candidate seems to have been saying one thing while the Vatican has been saying something quite different.

The Ripsaw (single sheet), P.O. Box 3002, Sta. B, South Bend, Ind. When one religion has power, it exterminates and per-

102

secutes all who oppose it. But there has never been any such record of slaughter by Rationalists and Freethinkers.

A Roman Catholic President? (21-page pamphlet), by Charles R. Andrews, pub. by American Baptist Convention, Council on Christian Social Progress, 152 Madison Ave., New York 16, N.Y. Singles out for consideration the confusing and conflicting views about the relationship between church and state expressed by Ryan and Boland in *Catholic Principles of Politics,* on the one hand and by Father John Courtney Murray and others on the other hand. The dilemma for the voter is to decide intelligently which of the two sides represents the long-range goal of a given candidate.

A Roman Catholic President? (leaflet), by Charles W. Conn, Church of God, 1080 Montgomery Ave., Cleveland, Tenn. Dr. Conn opposes the Catholic "system" and not any individual Catholic. The Catholic hierarchy does not believe in religious freedom for all because wherever Catholics dominate, they seek union of church and state and deny religious freedom.

A Roman Catholic President (12-page leaflet), by George L. Ford, exec. dir., National Association of Evangelicals, dist. by United Evangelical Action, 222 East Willow Ave., Wheaton, Ill. Theme: since the Roman Catholic Church chooses to make its play in the political arena, a Catholic President would work under serious limitations. Thus, the basic issue is not religion but the political action of the Roman Church. Religion is the means used to demand loyalty in order to put the political action into operation.

A Roman Catholic President? (9-page booklet), by Luther W. Martin, pub. by Bible School Press, Athens, Ala. Concerned with the political and temporal aspects of the Catholic Church. Sees a parallel between communism and Catholicism, and concludes that neither political party can afford to run a Catholic for President or Vice-President of the United States.

A Roman Catholic President? (4-page leaflet), pub. by New Jer-

103

sey Council of Christian Churches. The question is: "Do you want a president whose first allegiance would be to the Pope of Rome above his country, who would be used to make America Roman Catholic, and who would ignore the Constitution which guarantees freedom of religion and separation of church and state?"

A Roman Catholic President? (16-page booklet), by James M. Tolle, pub. by J. M. Tolle, 2046 Kearney St., Denver 7, Col. The author's thesis is that it would be impossible for a Catholic President to be loyal to the Roman Catholic Church and at the same time loyally serve all the American people, regardless of their religious beliefs, and do his part as the chief executive in supporting both the letter and the spirit of the Constitution. There is a basic conflict between the American way of life and Catholicism because the latter accepts the Constitutional guarantee of all religions before the law as a matter of expediency and not of principle.

A Roman Catholic for President? (3-page offset), by Jack Odom, Box 833, Fort Bragg, Cal. The theme is that Catholic subservience to the foreign despot of a monarchical, authoritarian, clerical, Fascist state, the Vatican, is incompatible with American democracy. If Kennedy is a good and devout Roman Catholic, he cannot be trusted as President, because the hierarchy would use him to direct and control the foreign and domestic affairs of our country.

A Roman Catholic President? A Documented Research Report on a Vital Issue (44-page booklet), by Philip McIlnay, 4638 15th Ave., South Minneapolis, Minn., 1960. Insists that American Catholicism is not different, and that if and when Roman Catholicism comes to power in our country, Protestants would probably be allowed to worship, although the building of churches would be limited. Theological seminaries might be closed; Roman Catholicism would be named the country's official religion; control of education, religion, and family relations would be transferred to the Catholic

104

hierarchy. Non-Catholics should be alert to Roman Catholic moves toward control in education, government, etc. Catholics should do something about the problem within their own church. The reality of the alleged danger of Catholic control is evidenced by trends in the last twelve years. About that length of time ago, Harold E. Fey, now editor of *The Christian Century*, completed a series of articles for that journal under the title "Can Catholicism Win America?" He concluded the series by answering in the affirmative, and every trend which he noticed has become more pronounced in the years since.

A Roman Catholic for President: The Strategy of the Vatican (6-page folder), by Joseph Zacchello, pub. by *The Convert* (*q.v.*). An answer to Sen. Paul Douglas's article "A Catholic Can Become President," *Coronet*, March, 1959. Zacchello claims that the Vatican strategy is a step-by-step affair since the country is not yet 51 percent Roman Catholic and so not ripe for a take-over. The first step is for Catholics to penetrate into every area of public life and make themselves felt. The second step is to impress the non-Roman Catholic people that a Catholic can safely be elected to any political job without fear that he will put loyalty to his church above loyalty to his duty of office. The article by Senator Douglas is supposed to prove that we are still on step two in the U.S. The hierarchy permitted Kennedy to publish a very liberal manifesto on religion, apparently accepting American democratic principles, as part of the strategy.

The Roman Catholic Syllabus and Vatican Decrees versus the Knights of Columbus Religious Information Bureau, by Foy E. Wallace, Jr. The K. of C. information program contradicts the *Syllabus* as part of the propaganda campaign to brainwash the American people.

Roman Catholicism and Our Next President (leaflet), sermon by Thomas Hansen, pastor, First Baptist Church, Fort Lauderdale, Fla., August 14, 1960. Courteous and Christian in tone,

105

but warns that religious liberty and the right to private judgment are denied to Baptists, Protestants, and all other Evangelicals in lands dominated by Roman Catholicism.

Roman Catholicism and the Presidency (7-page pamphlet), sermon by Gilbert M. Beenken, Oliver Presbyterian Church, 27th and Bloomington Ave., Minneapolis, Minn. This message is not directed against Roman Catholics but against Roman Catholicism, i.e., the hierarchy and the clericalism in the Church.

Roman Catholicism Under the Searchlight (16-page booklet), by Eugene M. Harrison, Ph.D., Wheaton, Ill. Extensively "documented" attack on the "stealthy and dangerous enemy, the Church of Rome" (p. 3). A dangerous threat to American freedom is constituted by this powerful and subversive foe, "clad in the garments of religion and equipped with all the tools in the arsenal of totalitarianism (p. 3). Concludes that Roman Catholicism, when subjected to the searchlight of the truth of history and of God's Word, turns out to be the church described prophetically as a wicked city, characterized by enormous wealth and worldly pomp.

Rome Today, Washington Tomorrow: Vatican Hopes (15-page booklet), speech by Ernesto Rossi, Eliseo Theater, Rome, June 11, 1960, translated and reprinted from *La Parola del popolo*, August–September, 1960. This is a warning to Americans about the dangers to democratic institutions which would be posed by a Catholic President. "Kennedy is not a liberal Catholic such as were the patriots of our 'Risorgimento' who defied all the Pope's anathemas and excommunications to abolish ecclesiastical privileges, combat abuses among the clergy, dissolve religious bodies and turn their property over to the State, overthrow the temporal power of the Papacy and establish in Rome the capital of Italy. Kennedy is . . . Cardinal Spellman's candidate" (p. 7). "If Kennedy declares that a Catholic president of the U.S. would not be required to obey the orders which he would receive, on political matters, from the Pope, this declaration, which for a Catholic is substantially heretical has been made with the connivance of Cardinal Spellman who knows that, when the occasion arises, he would be well able to persuade President Kennedy that in those matters which affect the Holy See, politics touch the altar and when politics touch the altar it is no longer politics but a matter of faith and morals in which the Pope is infallible; if a Catholic wishes to remain a Catholic, then he must obey without question the decision taken by the ecclesiastical hierarchy" (p. 7).

ROME'S RESPONSIBILITY FOR THE ASSASSINATION OF ABRAHAM LINCOLN and *Education—Is it Important?* (2 brochures), pub. by Heritage Manor, Inc., P.O. Box 75673, Sanford Sta., Los Angeles 5, Cal. The second brochure asserts that the number one enemy of the public schools is the Roman Catholic Church.

The Saints' Herald, July 11, 1960: "Dangers of Complacency," by Wallace Smith. Notes the fact that a statement was recently issued from the Vatican (*Osservatore Romano,* May 18, 1960) to the effect that Catholic leaders have not only the right but also the responsibility to guide the political thinking of the lay members of the Catholic Church everywhere. This includes the U.S.A.

SCOTTISH RITE OF THE MASONIC LODGE, Portland, Ore. A letter, "Election Call to Citizens," by Leslie M. Scott of Portland, Ore., dated October, 1960, to 6500 members in Oregon. Claims that the Roman Catholic priesthood seeks political power in America. If they gain it, there will be restriction and persecution. Kennedy is a loyal subject of the Vatican, and is bound by its mandates.

The Scottish Rite Torch (monthly magazine), Union Ave., Memphis, Tenn., September, 1960, p. 4: "Roman Catholic President?" and "Church Would Change the Constitution." Opposed to the control and supervision of free public schools by any church or ecclesiastic power, foreign or domestic.

Secularism (leaflet), by C. Stanley Lowell, assoc. dir. of Protestants and Other Americans United, Truth Series Leaflet No.

3, pub. by POAU, 1633 Massachusetts Ave., N.W., Washington 6, D.C. Denies that church-state separation means secularism, as the Roman Catholics claim it does. The real secularists, according to Lowell, "are those who try to put the church where it has no business to be—under the sponsorship and financial support of the state." Thus, the Roman Catholic Church has produced as much secularism as communism ever has. By infiltrating the government in, for example, Spain, Italy, Portugal, Argentina, and Colombia, it deliberately sullies and secularizes itself. It becomes an organization of self-seeking bureaucrats, living on funds furnished by the public, thinking more of its own power than of the people it is supposed to serve. In invading the secular order, the Church becomes secularized; it does not influence the state, but tries to use the state's coercive power for its own advantage. It does not make the state moral but becomes immoral itself.

Senator Kennedy's Oath of Office (leaflet), radio message by Emmet McLaughlin [sic], author of *People's Padre* and *American Culture and Catholic Schools,* given on the program "The Christian Forum" over Station KHEP, Phoenix, Ariz. In the light of Catholic teaching about mental reservation, any statement of a Catholic candidate that he is free of Rome is ignorance, wishful thinking, or a bold-faced lie. The Catholic Church insists that its laws are above the laws of every country, and every government official must give prior allegiance to the Church.

Shall a Roman Catholic Be President? (pamphlet), by J. B. Rowell, Th.D., portions of articles appearing in *Christian Heritage,* March and April, 1959, reprinted from *Sunday School Times,* 325 North 13th St., Philadelphia 5, Pa., February 6, 1960. Points out the incompatibility between Catholicism and American democracy. Notes the storm of protest in the "Romish press" over Senator Kennedy's 1959 *Look* article with the controversial statement: "Whatever one's re-

108

ligion in private life may be, for the office holder nothing
takes precedence over his oath to uphold the Constitution."

A Shocking Exposé from Official Catholic Documents (31-page
booklet), by O. C. Lambert, Winfield, Ala. Charges that
Roman Catholicism is un-American in that it desires a union
of church and state, and places the Pope over every human
creature and the Catholic Church over civil governments. Evidence is drawn from statements of the American hierarchy
and books printed in the United States.

*Should an Avowed Roman Catholic Be Elected President of the
U.S.?* (6-page folder), radio message by Joseph Lewis, given
over Station WMIE, Miami, Fla., January 30, 1960, dist. by
Freethinkers of America, 370 West 35th St., New York 1,
N.Y., a national nonprofit membership organization devoted
to the preservation of the constitutional provisions providing
for the separation of church and state. The main reason for
considering a Roman Catholic an exception to the "no religious test" provision of the Constitution is the fact that
Roman Catholicism places the Pope at the summit of a man's
loyalty, above his duty and obligation as a citizen of the
United States. The Constitution of the United States is a
secular document providing for church-state separation and
freedom of conscience for all. The Church of Rome is a religious organization that claims superiority over all governments and that it is the only true church, and demands absolute subservience of all peoples.

Should a Roman Catholic Be President? Would Liberties Be Lost?
(22-page booklet), by Dr. David Calderwood, pres., California Christian Citizens Association, 24215 Stanhurst Ave.,
Lomita, Cal., dist. by the Bible Baptist Church, Lincoln, Me.,
and also circulated at the Democratic National Convention.
States specifically that while there is no dislike for Roman
Catholics, there is opposition "to the system of government
in that church which is completely undemocratic, and, therefore, un-American, for the people have no voice whatsoever in

the choice of their rulers, nor in determining the church's articles of faith and the substance of its worship. They owe unquestioning obedience to an autocratic, self-perpetuating hierarchy" (pp. 5–6).

The Southerner (periodical), ed. by C. T. Pratt, Box 259, Dalton, Ga., July 14, 1960: "We Won't Vote for a Catholic," editorial. Pratt chides Protestants for being afraid to speak out against the very thing that they know will take away their freedom.

STANDISH, MRS. F. M., 1419 Clayton St., San Francisco, Cal. A 5-page letter, "Dear Friend," warns of the hierarchy's aim of getting control of this country and then making war on every non-Catholic country and our own "heretics." The "Potential Catholic Militia" for this enterprise would include the Catholic graduates of West Point, Annapolis, the Air Force Academy, employees of the F.B.I., members of the Congress, etc.

A Statement of Concern (paper), adopted by the Board of Administration of the National Association of Evangelicals, representing 38 denominations and 28,000 church congregations, at its midyear meeting at St. Louis, October 11, 1960: "The religious issue in the present political campaign has been distorted. It must be made clear that the mode of worship exercised by any candidate for public office is not in question. The manner of a man's approach to God must be a matter of his own choosing. Nevertheless, when an ecclesiastical system advocates the use of government to pursue its particular religious objectives and asserts that it has the right to control the political actions of its adherents, the religious issue must be considered by the voter. The record of the Roman Catholic Church on these two points, despite wishful thinking to the contrary, is a matter of history—fully documented and well known. Failure of the Roman Catholic hierarchy to repudiate and abandon this interference both in private conscience and in the political affairs of governments impels non-Catholics to register their position in the current campaign."

A Statement Regarding Electing a Roman Catholic to the Presidency, by Thomas F. Zimmerman, gen. supt., Assemblies of God, reprinted from *The Pentecostal Evangel*, 434 West Pacific St., Springfield, Mo. The Assemblies of God were born in protest, and must now work to prevent the highest position in the land from going to a member of the Roman Catholic Church. The position of President is different from that of governor or Senator because of its great prestige and power. A Catholic President could begin a major tide toward Roman Catholic control and direction of America through his appointments; and he would do so because every Roman Catholic is completely under the control of his Church, mind, soul, and body. The Assemblies of God spent fourteen years in a court battle in Italy, seeking religious freedom for their churches. They finally gained the right to public worship, but only because of pressure from the United States. This is the story in all lands where the Roman Catholic Church controls the government. It reflects the Catholic position on Protestantism as expressed, for example, in *Brownson's Quarterly Review*, XIV, p. 768: "Protestantism of every form has not and never can have any rights where Catholicity is triumphant."

A Statement of Principles (leaflet), by K. O. White, pastor, First Baptist Church, Houston, Tex. The principles concern the "hierarchy" which the Catholic candidate represents:

1. The Catholic Church is a state as well as a church.
2. It does not accept church-state separation.
3. It directs the lives of its members in political matters.
4. Roman Catholicism is concentrating on the U.S.
5. Election of a Catholic President would be a step toward domination in the U.S. as in other lands.

Stop Kennedy—Why? (yellow card), by Gerald L. K. Smith, dist. by Christian Nationalist Crusade, P.O. Box 27895, Los Angeles 27, Cal. The center of Smith's campaign against Kennedy. The seven reasons given on the back of the card are, in summary, (1) Kennedy is a permanent adolescent and (2) the scion of a whiskey trust; (3) he whitewashed Walter Reuther and his goons, (4) led in the repeal of the loyalty oath for students enjoying Federal subsidy, (5) opposed the anti-Communist crusade of the late Sen. Joseph McCarthy, and (6) advocated presidential apology to Khrushchev following the summit blow-up; and (7) he is the candidate of an overambitious father with unlimited wealth.

A Strategy of Action (leaflet), Truth Series Leaflet No. 12, pub. by Protestants and Other Americans United, 1633 Massachusetts Ave., N.W., Washington 6, D.C. The story of POAU and its beginnings in 1948 for the purpose of educating the public to the value of church-state separation. The main target of attack has been the use of tax funds for church enterprises. POAU claims that a new psychology was developing in the United States in the late 1940s. It grew out of a clever propaganda campaign to persuade people that it was the state's duty to provide financial support for church activity, and that if the state failed to do so it was "secularist" or "atheist."

Sunshine News (weekly publication), ed. by Paul Rader, Th.D., Litt.D., pub. by River Lake Tabernacle, Luke Rader, Th.D., D.D., founder, River Drive and Lake St., Minneapolis 6, Minn., August 25, 1960: "Kennedy and the Vatican: Religious Freedom," by Dr. W. A. Criswell.

The Sword of the Lord (weekly newspaper), Box 420, Wheaton, Ill., September 16, 1960: "Kennedy for President?", by Evangelist Robert L. Summer. Warns of the dangers involved.

Technocracy Briefs (1-page quarterly sheet), ed. by Cyril Large, 2208 Eighth Avenue., Seattle 1, Wash., October, 1954: "A Message to American Catholics." Technocracy is acclaimed as "non-religious," though not "anti-religious." It is opposed to the dual allegiance of Catholics and to their attempts to impose their censorship laws on others.

Ten Reasons Why Good Roman Catholics Should Vote for John Fitzgerald Kennedy for President of the United States (4-page leaflet), by Vernon M. Blikstad, pub. by Osterhus Publishing Co., 4500 West Broadway, Minneapolis 22, Minn. This piece was a dangerous fraud. It purported to be a Catholic exhortation to vote for Kennedy, but was, in fact, anti-Catholic. Blikstad, a Minneapolis insurance agent, was dropped by the Nixon-Lodge Volunteers in Minneapolis. The ten reasons are: (1) to break the Protestant monopoly on the White House; (2) to get state and federal support for our Catholic schools; (3) to make our Holy Mother Mary the true First Lady of the Land; (4) to get more fringe benefits for our church through foreign aid, hospital bills, free lunches, textbooks, and bus rides, and health benefits for Catholic school children; (5) to re-establish U.S. relations with Pope John XXIII and the Vatican; (6) to have more Catholics appointed to public jobs; and (7) to prevent the spread of birth-control information; (8) the tremendous prestige of a Catholic in the White House would help win to the Church other minorities—Negroes, Jews, Indians; (9) after a successful first term, President Kennedy could begin to get Catholic principles translated into civil law; and (10) most of our strength is in the cities, and we need fresh impetus for a drive to win traditionally Protestant rural America back to Christ. A lavish farm program would help break down prejudice. To win apostate America back to Mother Church, we must hurdle four high obstacles: the Constitution, the public school system, the Supreme Court, and the Protestant Church itself.

To All Who Love America and Religious Freedom (2 typewritten pages), by J. F. Murphy, "Free-thinking Catholic," Boston, Mass. A few years ago, the non-Catholic Democrats let the Catholic Democrats talk them into helping elect a Catholic governor. And so on down the line—you have to be a Catholic to get anywhere in Massachusetts. Can you imagine what a Catholic President would do to America? All key appointments would go to Catholics, for the Pope wants rich Amer-

113

ica under Catholic control. Keep the country free as it is now and not under any church control.

To Kill Protestants (leaflet), by Joseph Zacchello, pub. by *The Convert* (*q.v.*). The Roman Catholic Church still claims the right to kill heretics. This book *State and Church*, by Ryan and Millar, proves that the Catholic Church plans to impose her laws against heretics on this free country and to change the Constitution as soon as she is able to do so.

To "Wake Up Humanity" by Calling the World's Biggest Bluff (8 mimeographed pages), by George W. Adams, 3 Bay State Rd., Pittsfield, Mass. Addressed to editors in chief and colleagues of the Long Island Press, New York, this message in letter form warns that the Roman Catholic Church is doing everything in its subversive power to brainwash our voters into dodging the religious issue during elections. The Roman Catholic Church is anything but a religion. It fully represents "the most wicked crime conspiracy of all time!!!"

The Truth Seeker (magazine), 38 Park Row, New York, N.Y.: "What About a Catholic for President?", by Marshall J. Gauvin. The reasons for opposition to a Catholic candidate flow from the differences between Americanism and Catholicism: (1) the American people believe in absolute separation of church and state, but Catholics must believe in the union of the Catholic Church and the state; (2) the monstrous consequences of the doctrine of papal infallibility. In the whole range of its specific character, Catholicism as such is at war with the progressive spirit of the American people. But fortunately, there is something to be said on the other side. Thus, the character and platform of the candidate should be examined, and if these are approved, he should be voted for regardless of the religious beliefs he holds. "The modern world moves steadily toward the rationalization of religion and the secularization of social life. . . . I am satisfied that if Senator Kennedy wins the Democratic nomination and the Presidency, he will be loyal to his trust as an American" (p. 87).

Twelve Reasons Why I Will Not Vote for a Catholic for President of the United States (24-page booklet), by D. N. Jackson, LL.D., ed., *American Baptist*, P.O. Box 99, Jacksonville, Tex. (1) Kennedy's religion advocates a union of church and state; (2) it advocates the domination of the church over the state; (3) the Pope is a ruler who seeks to dominate the state; (4) the Pope is a kind of God on earth; (5) the Pope controls the thoughts and activities of individuals; (6) the Church aims to make America Catholic; (7) the Church aims to get public tax funds; (8) the Catholic Church is contrary to the U.S. Constitution; (9) the greater the influence of Catholicism in a country, the greater the possibility of a vacuum to be filled by communism; (10) Catholics are opposed to the public school system; (11) the Church has prohibitive marriage regulations; (12) the Catholic layman must depend on his superiors for his personal conduct.

UNITED CHURCH OF CHRIST, COUNCIL FOR CHRISTIAN SOCIAL CONCERN, 289 Park Ave., South, New York 10, N.Y. A letter by Huber F. Klemme, acting dir., dated October 1, 1960, to the ministers and members of Evangelical and Reformed and Congregational Christian Churches, restates the "Qualifications for the Office of the Presidency of the United States," issued on January 31, 1960. "The Council for Christian Social Concern unequivocally states its conviction that no citizen should be denied nomination by a political party or election to the office of President on grounds of race, religion, or ethnic origin." This does not mean that citizens may not ask questions about a presidential candidate's character, beliefs, and affiliations, including his religious beliefs and affiliations. Since the Roman Catholic Church is known to contain at least two opposing views of the preferred relationship between church and state and of the basis for religious liberty, it would be important to know the views of a Roman Catholic candidate on those issues. Religious affiliation must not automatically qualify or disqualify a citizen for any political office.

United Evangelical Action (monthly magazine), pub. at Newton, Kans., ed. by W. Stanley Mooneyham, P.O. Box 28, Wheaton, Ill., September, 1960, pp. 8–9: "Religious Freedom and the Presidency," by Dr. W. A. Criswell.

October, 1960, p. 8: "Capital Commentary," by Don Gill. The author, on leave as assistant secretary of public affairs for the National Association of Evangelicals, was named executive director of Citizens for Religious Freedom, formed as a result of the Washington conference in September, 1960. Gill writes in defense of the Conference, and against the press for hammering at Dr. Peale and making him the scapegoat by labeling it the "Peale Group." He insists that, at that time, the religious issue was not out in the open, that much fog still surrounded it, and that further discussion would show greater maturity by avoiding the kind of mudslinging then directed at Dr. Peale.

United Presbyterian Messenger (monthly), 308 Patterson Bldg., Omaha, Neb., October, 1960, pp. 2, 5: "Is This Bigotry?", by George S. Bancroft, ed. Raises the question of how a good Catholic who believes that the Pope is the voice of final truth can serve as the head of a state which holds the constitutional principle of separation of church and state.

Unlock Clubs Enter Presidential Religious Controversy (3-page mimeographed news release), by Jack Odom, Box 833, Fort Bragg, Cal., October 20, 1960. Rev. J. E. Hewlett, Baptist, St. Louis, Mo., a leader of the Unlock Clubs movement, is pictured showing the pin button that symbolizes the movement. The figure on the button is a closed padlock and the word UNLOCK. The wearer of the button explains that he will insist that the Roman Catholic Church unlock the Protestant church doors it has closed, and stop persecuting Protestants, before parading its claims upon American freedoms.

Vatican Refutes Look Magazine and Reverend O'Brien (11-page mimeographed packet), pub. by Heritage Manor, Inc., P.O. Box 75673 Sanford Sta., Los Angeles 5, Cal. A list of quota-

116

tions out of context from canon law, Catholic encyclopedia, the Popes, and other sources.

The Vindicator: Opposes Every False Doctrine—Vindicates Gospel Obedience (8-page newspaper), pub. by Dillard Thurman, 2800 South Bryan, Fort Worth, Tex., September, 1960: "The Vatican Speaks—Will the Pope Rule Us?" Repeats the charge of Vatican disregard for church-state separation.

"A Brigadier General Warns All America," by Brig. Gen. Herbert C. Holdridge (ret.). The warning is about the danger of Catholicism.

Voice of Freedom (monthly publication), ed. by L. R. Wilson, pub. by Freedom Press, P.O. Box 128, Nashville, Tenn., July, 1959): "Editorial." Catholics are as hard to understand as Communists. They ban birth control in spite of the fact of overpopulation. If we want communism to take over the United States, all we have to do is increase the population until it is dominated by Roman Catholicism, inferior schools, and unemployment.

November, 1959, p. 174: " 'Glamour' Candidates and the Dilemma of Dual Loyalty." Editor denies that any man can be loyal to the papacy and the United States at the same time.

September, 1960, pp. 131–132: "From the Editor's Viewpoint." Opposition to Senator Kennedy by the *Voice of Freedom* stems not only from his religion but also from the fact of his inexperience, ambition, and subservience to big labor bosses.

"Is He Fish or Fowl?", by the Washington correspondent. Kennedy's declaration of independence from Rome is called duplicity and a device to trick non-Catholics into believing that he is one of them.

October, 1960, pp. 147–148: "From the Editor's Viewpoint: Roman Catholicism is More Than a Religion." It is a combination of church and state.

The Voice of Healing (monthly magazine), ed. by Gordon Lindsay, 1600 Bonnie View Rd., P.O. Box 8658, Dallas, Tex., September, 1960: "Shall We Have a Catholic President?" by Gordon Lindsay and Harry Hampel. This is a question which threatens the religious freedom of our country. Many American Catholics are unaware of the history of the Roman Catholic system. They know nothing of its inherent religious intolerance, of its Inquisition, of the severe persecution of Protestants in many Catholic countries even today. The root of the trouble is the doctrine of papal infallibility, which makes it necessary for the Church to justify all its deeds of the past.

The W. C. Taylor Letters (periodical publication; 6 pages), Box 1504, Louisville, Ky., Letter No. 23: "What Is Roman Catholicism?" Taylor claims that *the* issue is the *free voter*, not the free candidate, because there has been a campaign to intimidate and browbeat the free voter who happens to think that Roman Catholicism in a candidate disqualifies him for the presidency. Catholics and others should not label as "bigots" and "prejudiced" all who vote against Kennedy. Where Catholics rule, non-Catholics are not even eligible to be candidates.

Wake Up, America!, pub. by Citizens' Committee, P.O. Box 148, Pitman, N.J. "Is A Loyal Son of the Church of Rome Qualified for Public Office in the United States of America????" Answers from Catholic sources show that he is not.

Warning Letter to Fellow Pilgrims on the Journey into the "World of the Unknown" Whither All of Us Are Bound, by Rev. Harrison Parker, Puritan Church of America, 1868 Columbia Rd., Washington 9, D.C. The aim is to arouse the sleeping Protestants to what Catholics are doing under cover of religious toleration.

Washington Under the Sway of Romanism! (16-page booklet), compiled by Rev. Angelo Di Domenica, D.D., pub. by Osterhus Publishing Co., 4500 West Broadway, Minneapolis 22, Minn. Contains photostatic copies of letters written in 1936 and 1937 by Rev. Patrick Henry O'Brien which supposedly demonstrate the intrigues and aspirations of the Roman Church in America.

118

Watchman-Examiner (Baptist weekly newspaper), September 15, 1960: "Religion and the U.S. Presidency," by Gordon Palmer, past president of Eastern Baptist Theological Seminary. Thinks that good Americans should be disturbed about the whole matter of having a Roman Catholic in the White House because of what the Roman Catholic hierarchy believe and practice. Protestants are firmly committed to the freedom guaranteed by the U.S. Constitution. *Immortale Dei* implies that while in the minority, the hierarchy submits to the rule of the Constitution, but when in a majority, they resume their intolerant dictatorship from which the Founding Fathers fled.

September 29, 1960, pp. 762–764: "The Catholic-Protestant Dilemma," by Sterling L. Price, pastor, Third Baptist Church, St. Louis, Mo. This is addressed to "Mr. Candidate," and expresses very well the concern of many Protestants about the intentions of the Catholic Church in the United States. Typical queries by Reverend Price: "Does it embarrass you when *America* criticizes your statement: 'A man's religion is a private matter,' by saying that this was not good Catholic doctrine? Protestants were made happy by your statements." "Does it embarrass you when the present pope, John XXIII, in May of this year gave a very clever reply and subtle rebuke to you for your statement about putting the Constitution of the U.S. above the Roman Catholic hierarchy? The *Osservatore Romano,* the official Vatican newspaper, quotes Pope John XXIII as having said this: 'The church has the right and the duty to guide, direct and correct. . . . A Catholic can never depart from the teachings and directives of the church, in every sector of his activities he must be motivated by the laws and instructions of the hierarchy. . . . The problem of collaboration with those who do not recognize religious principles might arise in a political field. It is then up to the ecclesiastical authorities, and not to the arbitrary decisions of individual Catholics, to judge the moral licitness of such collaboration.' " (It should be noted that the Pope was

119

not the author of this statement in *Osservatore Romano*, and that its publication at the time was deplored by the then Secretary of State Cardinal Tardini). Thus, according to Pastor Price, there is an apparent contradiction between the independence which Senator Kennedy is asserting and the "official" statements of his Church.

The Wealthiest Body in the World (4-page leaflet), by an anonymous converted Roman Catholic priest, pub. by Osterhus Publishing Co., 4500 West Broadway, Minneapolis 22, Minn. Claims that the property of the Roman Catholic Church is the most serious menace that threatens the existence of our country.

The Western Recorder (16-page magazine), ed. by C. R. Daley, Middletown, Ky., August 18, 1960: "Political Dilemma for Papists," by C. R. Daley. The dilemma is that if the Roman Catholic candidate wins because the Baptists do not object, they stand to regret it deeply. If he loses because the Baptists put up a fight, they will be blamed for his defeat.

Western Voice (4-page newspaper), ed. and pub. by Rev. Harvey H. Springer, Western Voice Publishing Co., 3168 South Broadway, Englewood, Col., November 3, 1960: "Bishops Order Catholic Vote!", by R. C. Merryman. Instances the fact of the Puerto Rican pastoral as a warning to Americans.

What Every American Should Know: Is Catholic Control Possible in America? (leaflet), pub. and dist. by Freedom, P.O. Box 35652, Dallas, Tex. This group does not represent any church or group of churches, but a temporary cooperative effort to preserve religious freedom. The writers say that they sincerely believe that electing a loyal Catholic to the highest office in the world cannot help but give additional power to a religious group which has already made serious breeches in the wall of separation between church and state in the United States. They are not opposed to the individual man, but to the system, which is both religious and political, and whose head is in a foreign nation.

What Is the Religious Issue in the Present Campaign? (4-page leaflet), address by Roy L. Laurin, D.D., 1499 Colorado Blvd., Los Angeles, Cal. The religious issue is the Roman Catholic position on (1) separation of church and state, (2) sectarianism in the public schools, (3) clericalism in the U.S., (4) pressure to obtain tax money to support sectarian institutions, (5) persecution of minorities, (6) the structure of the Church, and (7) the methods of achieving its goals.

Which Do You Choose? Liberty or Bigotry (cartoon), pub. in *Solidarity* (UAW publication), September 26, 1960. The implication drawn from the cartoon brought down sharp rebukes on the UAW, which in turn prompted a statement from President Walter Reuther expressing regret over the cartoon. This was followed by an editorial which made it clear that people were free to disagree with the political position taken by the UAW without being labeled bigots for doing so.

While America Sleeps (24-page pamphlet), by R. F. Becker, pub. by Christ's Mission, 369 Carpenter Ave., Sea Cliff, L.I., N.Y. Author claims that the Catholic Church is the "world's largest hydra-headed religio-political corporation, which has absolute control of billions of dollars worth of real estate in the U.S., completely tax exempt, while it takes every advantage of American liberty and freedom to further its relentless campaign to ruin the Democracy which protects it" (p. 3).

The White House: A Vatican Outpost (12-page pamphlet), by W. M. Montano, pub. by Christ's Mission, 369 Carpenter Ave., Sea Cliff, L.I., N.Y. In considering the possibility of a Roman Catholic President of the U.S., the American citizen must face the problem of an administration by a muzzled and harnessed Chief Executive, for a Roman Catholic does not have freedom to express an opinion on any subject.

Who Is a Bigot? (3 mimeographed pages), by H. S. Creger, Creger Hotel, Baytown, Tex. A warning to thoughtful Protestants that the history of the Catholic Church shows it to be an unchanging menace to American freedoms.

Who Is a Bigot? (leaflet), sermon by Dr. Herschel H. Hobbs, First Baptist Church, Oklahoma City, Okla., August 14, 1960. Claims that Protestant and especially Baptist reservations about Catholic political theories affecting religious freedom and the separation of church and state are not "bigotry" but the expression of deep-seated convictions growing out of the New Testament and historical experience. Dr. Hobbs evidently thinks that if America becomes Catholic-controlled, Baptists, other Protestants, and Jews would not long be allowed to conduct public worship services. Evidence: *Catholic Principles of Politics,* by Ryan and Boland, p. 317.

Who Says Refusal To Vote for a Roman Catholic Presidential Candidate Is Bigotry? (4-page leaflet), by Alexander O. Dunlap, pub. by the Conversion Center, Inc., 18 West Eagle Rd., Havertown, Pa. The Roman Catholic hierarchy is conducting a massive campaign to hide its true doctrines and to gain public sympathy. Hence, every American ought to examine Roman Catholic doctrines and canon law first hand. There is, for example, the doctrine of mental reservation, which could conveniently be used by a Roman Catholic presidential candidate. According to this doctrine, he could, for a sufficient reason, permit others to deceive themselves by taking the wrong meaning from what is said. There is also the *Syllabus* of Pius IX, which states: "The Church ought to be in union with the State, and the State with the Church." Further, the writings of Leo XIII, as set forth in Ryan's and Boland's *Catholic Principles of Politics,* proposes a program for making America Catholic.

Why Baptists and Protestants Fear a Catholic President, sermon by Dr. James E. Davidson, South Avondale Baptist Church, Birmingham, Ala., June 19, 1960, pub. in *The Alabama Baptist,* July 7, 1960, pp. 7–9. Says that the Baptist and Protestant opposition to a Roman Catholic President is not based on religious prejudice or the desire to persecute Roman Catholics. It is based on the avowed dogmas of that Church

122

and the well-known performance of the Church when it has had control of government. Intelligent voters should seriously ponder several questions before giving their support to a Catholic for President: (1) Catholic political designs and genius, (2) the "conflict of interest" issue involving church directives and U.S. civil practice, (3) the Catholic position on separation of church and state, (4) the fact that religious freedom is not a value for the Roman Catholic hierarchy except when they are in danger of losing it themselves, and (5) a sympathetic explosion of public displays of the Roman Catholic faith.

Why I Cannot now Vote for a Roman Catholic for President (23-page pamphlet), sermon by Dr. Harold A. Bosley, First Methodist Church, 1630 Hinman Ave., Evanston, Ill., February 28, 1960. Bosley states that his anxiety is rooted in one fact: ". . . the ambiguities if not outright contradictions which exist in Roman Catholic thought on both the principle and the practice of separation of Church and State and the meaning of religious freedom. So long as these exist, I cannot with confidence vote for a member of that Church as President of the United States" (p. 12). He sees as the official position on church and state the one expressed by Ryan and Millar, and finds another "unofficial" position suggested by various American spokesmen, e.g., Father J. C. Murray, S.J. Until 1940, Bosley was hopeful for harmonious interreligious relations in the U.S., but five major clashes in the past twenty years have disheartened him: (1) in 1939, the question of Roosevelt's appointment of Myron Taylor as his personal representative at the Vatican; (2) the effort of American Catholic Bishops to have non-Catholic missionaries withdrawn from Latin America; (3) the drive for aid to parochial schools; (4) Truman's attempt in 1951 to name Mark Clark ambassador to the Vatican; and (5) the steadily worsening relations between the Roman Catholic and other churches.

Why Not a Catholic for President—Would You Like the Pope of

Rome to Rule Over America?, dist. by the Voltaire Society, Box 7954, Chicago 80, Ill.

Why Not a Roman Catholic President? (1-page tract), by Evangelist C. William Fisher, reprinted from *Herald of Holiness,* Beacon Hill Press, 2923 Troost, Box 527, Kansas City 41, Mo., issue of March 30, 1960. The theme is that American Catholics are not really different but are members of an "ecclesiastical system"—a religious and political system—so rigid, so authoritarian, and so totalitarian that it demands and gets the first allegiance of every true member.

Why Not a Roman Catholic President? A Plea for Tolerance and Religious Liberty (leaflet), by Stephen L. Testa, minister of the Gospel, founder of the Scripture Truth Society and the Messenger of Christ Missionary Society, 5166 Ruthelen St., Los Angeles 62, Cal. Testa was formerly a Catholic, and his objection is on religious grounds rather than on political grounds—as Blanshard, POAU, and others. Wants to win converts from Catholicism. Is not in favor of a Catholic President, but deplores anti-Catholic propaganda, which he says will not sway the majority of Protestants who are fair-minded.

Why the Religious Issue? (8-page booklet), pub. by Houston Citizens Council for Separation of Church and State, P.O. Box 1797, Houston 1, Tex. Concludes that in the "light of the present policies and laws of the Roman Catholic Church, the bloody history of the Roman Catholic Church, and the intolerant and totalitarian structure of the Roman Catholic Church, there is only one course of action for the free and liberty loving man; that is uncompromising, steadfast opposition to this monstrosity of duplicity and mental slavery, the Roman Catholic hierarchy."

Why You May Lose Your Religious Liberty (4-page pamphlet), by Herbert H. Holland, Sr., pub. by AC Publications, 10 Fayette St., Concord, N.H. Claims that our religious liberty is seriously threatened by the lethargy of Protestants and the political scheming of the Roman Catholic hierarchy. The latter has never repudiated the right to suppress all opinions at variance with the dogmas of the "infallible" Church and Pope.

Will the Pope Move His Controlling System to the U.S.A.? Yes, If We Elect a Catholic for President of the U.S.A. (4-page leaflet), pub. by the Church of Jesus Christ, P.O. Box 21104, Houston, Tex. Predicts dire things for American freedom in a few years if we elect a Catholic for President. It will be against the law to say anything against the Pope or the Roman Catholic Church. There will be but one church, the Roman Catholic. Nuns will teach your children. There will be no freedom of the press, no freedom for the Protestant churches. The Roman Catholic hierarchy is Fascist.

World Evangelism (booklet), by John E. Douglas, Sr., P.O. Box 4326, Dallas 8, Tex., September, 1960. In any country controlled by Catholics, the people cannot enjoy the freedoms guaranteed in the U.S. Constitution. Even today, Catholics persecute the Christians in Latin American countries. The Roman Catholic Church, by her false propaganda, is regaining the power lost during the Reformation.

Would a Catholic President Put America First? (8-page pamphlet), by Hugh Malcolm, Enid, Okla., pub. by Defenders, Inc., Wichita 1, Kan. Singles out fear of the Church as the overriding issue in the election. The crucial question: "Would Senator John F. Kennedy or any other Catholic President do what he says he will do, or would he yield to the hierarchy in Rome when the chips were down?" (p. 2). Catholics do not really accept church-state separation.

Your Church and Your Candidate (4-page pamphlet), by Rev. Stuart P. Garver, pub. as Christian Heritage Pamphlet, Series P, by Christ's Mission, Box 925, Sea Cliff, L.I., N.Y. Warns of Church authority in the political field as evidenced by papal prohibition against Catholics' voting for parties which support the Communists and by the article *"Punti Fermi"* in *Osservatore Romano,* May 18, 1960. American Catholics are thus denied the unrestricted use of their constitutional freedoms.

125

Bibliography

THE FOLLOWING is a select list of books, articles, addresses, statements, and other materials related to the religious issue in the 1960 presidential election.

BOOKS

BENDINER, ROBERT, *White House Fever: An Innocent's Guide to Principles and Practices, Respectable and Otherwise, Behind the Election of American Presidents,* New York, Harcourt, Brace, 1960.

BENNETT, JOHN C., *Christians and the State,* New York, Scribner's, 1959.

BERELSON, BERNARD, Paul Lazarsfeld, and William McPhee, *Voting,* Chicago, University of Chicago Press, 1954.

BRANT, IRVING, *James Madison: Father of the Constitution, 1787–1800,* New York, Bobbs-Merrill, 1950.

BROGAN, D. W., *The American Character,* New York, Knopf, 1944.

BROGAN, D. W., *Politics in America,* New York, Harper, 1954.

BROWN, ROBERT MCAFEE, *The Spirit of Protestantism,* New York, Oxford University Press, 1961.

BURNS, JAMES MACGREGOR, *John Kennedy: A Political Profile,* New York, Harcourt, Brace, 1959.

CAMPBELL, ANGUS, Philip E. Converse, Warren E. Miller, and Donald E. Stokes, *The American Voter,* New York, Wiley, 1960.

DAVID, PAUL T., ed., *The Presidential Election and Transition 1960–1961,* Washington, Brookings, 1961.

D'ARCY, ERIC, *Conscience and Its Right to Freedom,* New York, Sheed & Ward, 1961.

DE ALBORNOZ, A. F. CARRILLO, *Roman Catholicism and Religious Liberty,* Geneva, World Council of Churches, 1959.

DULCE, BERTON, and E. F. Richter, *Religion and the Presidency,* New York, Macmillan, 1962.

ELLIS, JOHN TRACY, *American Catholicism,* Chicago, University of Chicago Press, 1956.

FELLMAN, DAVID, *The Limits of Freedom,* New Brunswick, Rutgers University Press, 1959.

FENTON, JOHN H., *The Catholic Vote,* New Orleans, Hauser, 1960.

GURIAN, WALDEMAR, and M. A. Fitzsimons, eds., *The Catholic Church in World Affairs,* South Bend, University of Notre Dame Press, 1954, especially the chapter "On the Structure of the Church-State Problem," by John Courtney Murray, S.J.

KELLY, STANLEY, JR., *Political Campaigning: Problems in Creating an Informed Electorate,* Washington, Brookings, 1960.

KERWIN, JEROME G., *Catholic Viewpoint on Church and State,* New York, Doubleday, 1960.

KURLAND, PHILIP B., *Religion and the Law,* Chicago, Aldine, 1962.

LANE, ROBERT, *Political Life: Why People Get Involved in Politics,* Glencoe, Free Press, 1959.

LEKACHMAN, ROBERT, *et al., The Churches and the Public,* Santa Barbara, Center for the Study of Democratic Institutions, 1960.

LENSKI, GERHARD, *The Religious Factor,* New York, Doubleday, 1961.

LITTELL, FRANKLIN H., *From State Church to Pluralism,* New York, Doubleday (Anchor), 1962.

MICHENER, JAMES A., *Report of the County Chairman,* New York, Random House, 1961.

MILLER, WILLIAM L., *et al., Religion and the Free Society,* New York, Fund for the Republic, 1958.

MURRAY, JOHN COURTNEY, S.J., *We Hold These Truths,* New York, Sheed & Ward, 1960.

ODEGARD, PETER H., ed., *Religion and Politics*, pub. for the Eagleton Institute of Politics, Rutgers University; Dobbs Ferry, Oceana, 1960.

PIKE, JAMES A., and Richard Byfield, *Roman Catholic in the White House*, Toronto, Doubleday, 1960.

RAFTON, HAROLD R., *What Do Roman Catholic Colleges Teach?* (a review of Ryan and Boland, *Catholic Principles of Politics*), Boston, Beacon, 1953.

ROSEN, ROBERTA, *A Roman Catholic Runs for President: A Comparison of the Anti-Catholic Literature in the Nineteenth Century and in the Presidential Campaigns of 1928 and 1960*, M.A. thesis, Smith College, April, 1961.

ROY, RALPH LORD, *Apostles of Discord: A Study of Organized Bigotry and Disruption on the Fringes of Protestantism*, Boston, Beacon, 1953.

STOKES, ANSON P., *Church and State in the United States*, New York, Harper, 1950, 3 vols.

TUSSMAN, JOSEPH, ed., *The Supreme Court on Church and State*, New York, Oxford University Press, 1962.

WHITE, THEODORE H., *The Making of the President, 1960*, New York, Atheneum, 1961.

ZAHN, JANE, ed., *Religion and the Face of America*, Berkeley, University of California Press, 1959.

PERIODICALS

AMERICA, March 7, 1959, p. 651: "On Questioning Catholic Candidates."

April 23, 1960, pp. 94, 96: "On Catholics and Other Candidates."

June 4, 1960, pp. 337–338: George Kelley, "Catholics: In 1960 and Later."

June 25, 1960, pp. 390–391: "A Bewildering Article."

July 9, 1960, p. 437: Donald McDonald, "A Theology of Toleration."

September 10, 1960, p. 606: "To Bigotry, No Sanction."

September 24, 1960, p. 689: "No Time for Anger."

pp. 690–695: "On Religious Toleration."

pp. 697–699: La Salle Woelfel, C.S.C., "The Oldest American Prejudice."

pp. 700–701: George Kelley, "A Time for Keeping On of Shirts."

pp. 702–708: "On Raising the Religious Issue: A Symposium." Contributors: Wayne H. Cowan, David Danzig, Rabbi Arthur Gilbert, Robert G. Hoyt, Jerome G. Kerwin, Robert Michaelsen, and John Courtney Murray, S.J.

November 5, 1960, pp. 163–165: "Puerto Rican Pastoral."

pp. 168–170: Glenn Tinder, "The Campaign and the Plight of Modern Society."

pp. 171–175: "Opinion Worth Nothing." Digest of Robert G. Hoyt, "The Religious Issue and Senator Kennedy," *Catholic Reporter*, October 28, 1960.

November 12, 1960, p. 198: "Reformation Sunday."

November 19, 1960, p. 257: "The People's Choice."

November 26, 1960, p. 290: "Amen, Brother!"

January 14, 1961, pp. 458–465: "What Hopes and What Misgivings Do You Entertain Regarding the Currently Emerging Religious Dialogue in America?" An exchange of views among Christian writers: John C. Bennett, Raymond T. Bosler, Robert M. Brown, Avery Dulles, S.J., Georges Florovsky, William L. Miller, John C. Murray, S.J., Philip Scharper, John B. Sheerin, C.S.P., Kenneth Underwood, Cyril Vollert, S.J., and the Most Rev. John Wright.

March 25, 1961, pp. 804–805: Francis Canavan, S.J., "Politics and Constitutional Law."

pp. 818–820: James J. Murray, "What Is the Real Issue?"

April 1, 1961, pp. 17–19: Charles M. Whelan, "School Question: Stage Two."

June 17, 1961, pp. 440–441: "A Public Purpose."

August 26, 1961, pp. 662–663: "Interview with Congressman Delaney."

AMERICAN BENEDICTINE REVIEW, March–June, 1960, pp. 1–20: John Tracy Ellis, "American Catholicism in 1960: An Historical Perspective."

AMERICAN CHRISTIAN REVIEW, November, 1960, pp. 2–3: "Our Country's 'New Foreign Policy.'"

AMERICAN ECCLESIASTICAL REVIEW, January, 1961, pp. 1–13: Francis J. Connell, C.SS.R., "Now That the Election Is Over."

AMERICAN FEDERATIONIST, October, 1960, pp. 3–7: Willard Shelton, "The Presidency."

December, 1960, pp. 3–8: Willard Shelton, "The How and Why of Kennedy's Victory."

AMERICAN JUDAISM, April, 1961, pp. 6, 30–31: John Wicklein, "Religious Issue Revisited."

AMERICAN POLITICAL SCIENCE REVIEW, June, 1961, pp. 269–280: Philip E. Converse, Angus Campbell, Warren E. Miller, and Donald E. Stokes, "Stability and Change in 1960: A Reinstating Election."

AMERICAN QUARTERLY, Summer, 1961, pp. 172–178: David O. Moberg, "Religion and Society in the Netherlands and in America."

ADL BULLETIN (pub. by the Anti-Defamation League of B'nai B'rith), April, 1960, pp. 1–2, 7–8: Bruce L. Felknor, "Warning From Wisconsin."

November, 1960, pp. 1–2, 6: Arnold Foster, "No Religious Test Shall Be Required. . . ."

AVE MARIA, May 28, 1960, pp. 5–8: Philip Scharper, "Why Protestants Fear Us."

BLACKFRIARS, June, 1960, pp. 207–219: J. M. Cameron, "Catholicism and Political Mythology."

BUSINESS WEEK, November 12, 1960, pp. 25–27: "The Democratic Victory: How Kennedy Won."

CAROLINA ISRAELITE, September-October, 1960, p. 4: Harry Golden, "An Answer to Dr. Norman Vincent Peale."

CATHOLIC LAWYER, Summer, 1961, pp. 183–202: William J. Kenealy, S.J., "Equal Justice Under Law—Tax Aid to Education."

CATHOLIC REPORTER, October 28, 1960 (special supplement), pp. 1–8: Robert Hoyt, "An Interpretation of the 'Religious Issue.'"

CATHOLIC WORLD, August, 1960, pp. 277–282: Bonaventure M. Schepers, O.P., "Catholic and Protestant Rules for Dialogue."

October, 1960, pp. 9–14: L. H. Fuchs, "Religious Vote, Fact or Fiction?"

December, 1960, pp. 132–136: John B. Sheerin, C.S.P., "The Embarrassing Puerto Rican Pastoral."

December, 1960, pp. 137–142: Joseph H. Crehan, S.J., "Thomists Discuss Tolerance."

December, 1960, pp. 143–148: Richard J. Regan, S.J., "Do Sunday Laws Restrict Religious Freedom?"

CHAPLAIN, October, 1960 (special issue on "Protestant-Roman Catholic Dialogue"), pp. 19–31: C. Emanuel Carlson, "Levels of the Dialogue."

CHRISTIAN CENTURY, February 3, 1960, pp. 133–135: Robert Michaelsen, "Religion and the Presidency, I."

February 10, 1960, pp. 159–161: "Robert Michaelsen, "Religion and the Presidency, II."

April 27, 1960, p. 499: "Moratorium on Bigotry."

July 6, 1960, pp. 799–800: Richard L. Means, "Perspective on the Population Issue."

July 20, 1960, p. 844: "Roman Catholic Church Enters Politics."

pp. 850–852: Thomas J. Liggett, "Protestantism in Puerto Rico."

August 17, 1960, pp. 939–940: "Religious Affiliation."

pp. 946–947: Warren B. Martin, "Weak Christian: Strong President."

131

September 7, 1960, p. 1013: "James W. Wine Becomes Kennedy's Aide."

September 14, 1960, pp. 1050–1052: A. Roy Eckardt, "When Is Faith Not Faith?"

September 21, 1960, pp. 1075–1077: "Religious Smoke Screen."

October 12, 1960, pp. 1181–1182: Michael Daves, "Religious Fracas in Dallas."

October 19, 1960, pp. 1212–1214: John W. Dykstra, "Catholics as a Pluralistic Minority."

   pp. 1214–1215: Elisha Greifer, "A Man from Mars for President?"

October 26, 1960, pp. 1235–1236: "Reformation and Election."

   pp. 1241–1243: Charles R. Andrews, "A Catholic President: Pro."

   pp. 1244–1247: Harold A. Bosley, "A Catholic President: Con."

November 2, 1960, pp. 1267–1268: "Morality and Politics."

November 9, 1960, pp. 1299–1300: "Issues That Abide."

November 16, 1960, p. 1331: "Responsible Government."

November 30, 1960, pp. 1402–1403: Eugene E. Crommett, "Vivan Los Populares!"

January 11, 1961, pp. 35–36: "Wall or Wavy Line?"

January 18, 1961, pp. 72–75: Martin Marty, "Protestantism Enters Third Phase."

January 25, 1961, pp. 93–94: "Protestant-Catholic Dialogue."

February 1, 1961, p. 147: John Garrett, "Open Letter to President Kennedy."

February 1, 1961, pp. 131–132: "A Regrettable Revival."

April 5, 1961, pp. 411–412: "Church Flexes Muscles."

April 5, 1961, pp. 415–417: Philip Burton, "Public Funds for Public Schools Only."

CHRISTIAN DEMOCRAT, May, 1961, pp. 221–229: "The Church in a Plural Society." Extracts from a pastoral letter issued by

Cardinal Rugambwa and the archbishops and bishops of Tanganyika.

CHRISTIAN HERALD, December, 1960, p. 6: Daniel Poling, "Election: Religion."

CHRISTIANITY AND CRISIS, March 16, 1959, pp. 25–26: Robert McAfee Brown, "Senator Kennedy's Statement."

August 3, 1959, pp. 115–117: Henry P. Van Dusen, "American Catholicism: Grounds for Misgivings."

pp. 117–118: Claud Nelson, "The Dialogue Continued."

March 7, 1960, pp. 17–19: John C. Bennett, "A Roman Catholic for President?"

September 19, 1960, pp. 125–126: John C. Bennett, "The Roman Catholic 'Issue' Again."

October 3, 1960, pp. 136–138, 140: Daniel J. Callahan, "Freedom and Authority in Roman Catholicism."

October 17, 1960, pp. 145–148: Eugene J. McCarthy, "Why I Will Vote Democratic."

pp. 148–151: Kenneth B. Keating, "Why I Will Vote Republican."

November 14, 1960, pp. 161–163: Roger L. Shinn, "What the Campaign Did to Religion."

November 28, 1960, pp. 170–171: John C. Bennett, "Triumph for American Democracy."

September 18, 1961, pp. 154–157: Harry L. Stearns, "Shared Time: Answer to an Impasse?"

pp. 157–160: Joseph E. Cunneen, "Parochial Schools and the National Common Good."

February 5, 1962, pp. 3–7: Will Herberg, "Protestantism in a Post-Protestant America."

pp. 7–10: Paul Lehmann, "Protestantism in a Post-Christian World."

May 28, 1962 (special issue on "Aid to Education"), p. 79: John C. Bennett, "The Debate on Education and Religion."

pp. 81–84: Maurice Rosenblatt, "Federal Aid to Education."

pp. 84–87: James E. McClellan, "Needed: A New Philosophy of Parochial Education."

pp. 88–91: Robert W. Lynn, "Impasse in Protestant Educational Strategy."

pp. 91–95: Thomas G. Sanders, "The Parental Right in Education."

CHRISTIANITY TODAY, January 4, 1960, pp. 20–22: "Taxation and the Churches."

May 9, 1960, p. 33: "The Big Debate: A Catholic President."

October 24, 1960, pp. 3–4, 11: C. Stanley Lowell, "The Protestant-Catholic Dialogue."

November 21, 1960, pp. 21–22: "Another Era Underway in the American Venture."

December 5, 1960, pp. 22–24: "Year's End: A Sound of Battle."

COMMENTARY, October, 1960, pp. 277–285: Arthur Hertzberg, "The Protestant 'Establishment,' Catholic Dogma, and the Presidency."

January, 1961, pp. 46–51: David Danzig, "Christianity in a 'Post-Western' Era."

May, 1961, pp. 428–432: Roma Lipsky, "Electioneering Among the Minorities."

August, 1961, pp. 93–104: Alan F. Westin, "The John Birch Society: Fundamentalism on the Right."

April, 1962, pp. 291–298: David Danzig, "The Radical Right and the Rise of the Fundamentalist Minority."

COMMONWEAL, May 6, 1960, pp. 140–141: "Bigotry and Responsibility."

May 13, 1960, pp. 164–165: "Discussion of Blake and Oxnam."

June 3, 1960, pp. 244–245: " 'L'Osservatore' on Politics."

June 24, 1960, pp. 317–318: "Reactions to 'L'Osservatore.' "

July 8, 1960, p. 350: John Cogley, "Religious People."

July 22, 1960, pp. 375–377: P. Simon, "Catholicism and the Elections."

August 5, 1960, pp. 387–388: "Religion in the Campaign."

September 2, 1960, pp. 435–436: "When Is an Issue?"

September 9, 1960, pp. 460–461: "Freed from Logic."

September 16, 1960, pp. 483–484: "And Now the Campaign."

pp. 491–494: Raymond F. Cour, "Catholics in Public Office."

September 23, 1960, pp. 507–508: "Catholicism and the paign."

pp. 509–510: "Statement of Principle."

pp. 517–518: David Danzig, "Bigotry and the Presidency."

September 30, 1960, pp. 5–6: "Catholic Opposition to Bigotry."

pp. 11–13: Arthur Moore, "Protestant Positions on a Catholic in the White House."

October 7, 1960, p. 30: "Degrees of Authority."

October 28, 1960, pp. 109–110: "Catholic Incongruity?"

November 4, 1960, pp. 139–140: "Puerto Rican Pastoral."

pp. 141–142: "Freedoms, Political and Religious."

January 26, 1962, pp. 451–454: Justus George Lawler, "Federal Aid and Freedom."

February 9, 1962, pp. 503–504: "The Church and Mr. Kennedy."

February 23, 1962, pp. 553–554: "Federal Aid: Second Round."

March 2, 1962, p. 586: James O'Gara, "Sharing the Time."

pp. 594–596: "Federal Aid and Freedom: An Exchange of Views."

April 6, 1962, pp. 36–38: "Federal Aid: Second Round."

CORONET, March, 1959, pp. 104–111: Paul Douglas, "A Catholic Can Become President!"

CROSS CURRENTS, Fall, 1960, pp. 313–316: Joseph Cunneen, "The Religious Issue and the Limits of National Purpose."

Summer, 1961, pp. 241–254: Yves M. J. Congar, O.P. "The Council, the Church and the 'Others.'"

135

ECONOMIST, October, 1960, pp. 45–46: "Party Loyalty—Texas Style."

November 5, 1960, pp. 545–556: "America's Choice."

November 12, 1960, pp. 653–654: "American Survey—Ambiguous Answer."

ECUMENICAL REVIEW, July, 1961, pp. 477–488: A. F. Carrillo De Albornoz, "Ecumenical Chronicle: Religious Liberty from Day to Day."

EDITORIAL RESEARCH REPORTS, September 9, 1959, pp. 673–694: Norman I. Gelman, "Religion in Politics."

ETHICAL OUTLOOK, November-December, 1960, pp. 198–202: Joseph L. Blau, "Religion and Culture in America."

FACTS (pub. by the Anti-Defamation League of B'nai B'rith), June–July, 1960, pp. 151–160: "The Religious Issue in the Presidential Campaign."

March 1961, pp. 185–200: "The 1960 Election Campaign."

GEORGETOWN LAW JOURNAL, Winter, 1961, pp. 399–455: National Catholic Welfare Conference, Legal Department, "The Constitutionality of the Inclusion of Church-Related Schools in Federal Aid to Education."

HARPER'S, January, 1961, pp. 53–57: Thomas B. Morgan, "The People-Machine."

HOMILETIC AND PASTORAL REVIEW, September, 1960, pp. 1121–1134: Leslie Rumble, M.S.C., "Pitfalls of Pluralism."

pp. 1134–1140: John A. Hardon, S.J., "A Catholic in the White House."

November, 1960, pp. 129–138: Virgil C. Blum, S.J., "Civil Rights for Children of Independent Schools?"

HUMAN EVENTS, April 7, 1961, pp. 213–216: Willard Edwards, "Did Biased Reporters Cost Nixon the Election?"

INFORMATIONS CATHOLIQUES INTERNATIONALES, October 15, 1960, pp. 15–25: "Les Nations Unies et la Liberté Religieuse."

November, 1960, pp. 17–28: Robert Hoyt, "Pour ou Contre un Président Catholique."

February 1, 1961, pp. 31–32: *"Lettre des U.S.A.—La Fin du 'Ghetto.'"*

INTERCHURCH NEWS, September, 1960, p. 2: "The Larger View." October, 1960, p. 2: "What Others Are Saying."

JEWISH FORUM, July, 1960, pp. 100–101: "Does Religion Influence Voting in America?"

JEWISH FRONTIER, October, 1960, pp. 8–11: Albert Vorspan, "Jewish Voters and the Religious Issue."

JEWISH LEDGER, August 4, 1960: Rabbi Jacob Neusner, "Religion and Politics."

JOURNAL OF CHURCH AND STATE, May, 1961, pp. 33–40: Richard C. C. Kim, "A Roman Catholic President in the American Schema."

JOURNAL OF PUBLIC LAW, VIII (1959), pp. 83–108: Joseph L. Costanzo, S.J., "Thomas Jefferson, Religious Education and Public Law."

JUBILEE, December, 1960, pp. 13–15: Robert Hoyt, "Kennedy, Catholicism and the Presidency."

JUDAISM, Fall, 1960, pp. 307–318: Malcolm Diamond, "The Emerging Dialogue."

LIFE, December 21, 1959, pp. 78–80+: James A. Pike, "Should a Catholic Be President?"

July 4, 1960, pp. 78–86: Robert Coughlan, "The Religious Issue: An Un-American Heritage."

September, 1960, p. 42: "Catholic Faces His Protestant Clerical Questioners."

October 31, 1960, p. 27: "Two-Sided Religious Issue."

LIVING CHURCH, September 25, 1960, pp. 16–17: "The Religious Issue."

LOOK, March 3, 1959, pp. 13–17: Fletcher Knebel, "Democratic Forecast: A Catholic in 1960."

February 16, 1960, pp. 17–21: John A. O'Brien, "Can Catholics Separate Church and State?"

May 10, 1960, pp. 31–34: Eugene C. Blake and G. B. Oxnam, "A Protestant View of a Catholic for President."

137

MEMPHIS PRESS-SCIMITAR, October 7, 1960: William H. Slavick, "Kennedy Has Met Every Test—Pollard's Charge Ridiculous."

October 19, 1960: James Claiborne, Jack Dicken, J. Kirk Graves, Joe L. McMillin, and James E. Threlkeld, "As Southern Baptists, Saddened by Attack on Catholics, We Feel Christians Need to Unite" (letter to the editor).

MIDSTREAM, Summer, 1960, pp. 5–15: Judd L. Teller, "The Jewish Vote—Myth or Fact?"

NEW LEADER, November 9, 1959, pp. 11–14: Lewis S. Feuer, "The Presidency and the Church."

pp. 14–15: George N. Shuster, "A Catholic Layman Replies."

November 23, 1959, p. 11: Richard S. Mowrer, "Spain Still Plagues Protestants."

May 9, 1960, pp. 3–4: Reinhold Niebuhr, "Catholics and the Presidency."

December 12, 1960, pp. 3–4: Reinhold Niebuhr, "The Religious Issue."

March 20, 1961, pp. 8–9: Reinhold Niebuhr, "School Aid, the President and the Hierarchy."

p. 10: William E. Bohn, "American Unity and the Problem of Federal Aid to Education."

April 17, 1961, pp. 3–5: Tristram Coffin, "The Yahoo Returns."

NEW REPUBLIC, March 21, 1960, pp. 3–16: "Catholics in America: Some Facts and Opinions Pertinent to the 1960 Campaign" (editorials, book review, and excerpts from letters and articles which appeared in the New Republic, January–March, 1960).

pp. 3–5: "Church and State" (editorial).

pp. 5–7: William Clancy, "Paul Blanshard Returns to His Subject."

p. 7: Paul Blanshard, "I Am an Ordinary Liberal Democrat."

p. 8: William Clancy, "A Profound Distrust of Catholic Intentions Exists."

pp. 9–10: "The Response of Some Readers" (excerpts from letters).

pp. 10–11: "The Catholic Issue" (editorial).

pp. 12–16: John Bennett, Arthur Schlesinger, Jr., and Jaroslav Pelikan, "Catholics in America."

November 14, 1960, p. 7: "Widening the Margin."

March 20, 1961, p. 2: T.R.B., "The School Issue."

pp. 3–5: "Parochial and Public."

April 24, 1961, p. 2: "The Anti-Catholic Vote."

NEW STATESMAN, September 24, 1960, p. 411: Robert Bendiner, "No Popery."

November 5, 1960, pp. 681–682: Robert Bendiner, "The Choice Before America."

NEWSWEEK, October 31, 1960, p. 21: "Sticky 'Issue.'"

NEW YORK HERALD TRIBUNE, October 16, 1960, pp. 1, 40: Robert S. Bird and Jo-Ann Price, "All-out Religious Attack on Kennedy Planned by 38 Fundamentalist Sects."

May, 1961: Terry Ferrer, education ed., "Crisis in the Catholic Schools" (10-page pamphlet reprint).

NEW YORK TIMES, October 17, 1960, p. 24: "Anti-Catholic Groups Closely Cooperate in Mail Campaign to Defeat Kennedy."

October 29, 1960, p. 12: Damon Stetson, "Prelate Defends Puerto Rican Ban."

November 20, 1960: Cabell Phillips, "About the Election: A Second Look."

OCCASIONAL BULLETIN (pub. by Missionary Research Library, 3041 Broadway, New York 27, N.Y.),

July 15, 1959, pp. 1–19: M. Searle Bates, "Religious Liberty —Church and State" (essay and a selected list of books).

OHIO JEWISH CHRONICLE, November 4, 1960, p. 2: Richard E. Neustadt, "Religious Issue."

OKLAHOMA COURIER, September, 1960, pp. 1–2: James Mc-Namee, "Church and State: An Explanation of the Catholic Position on Church and State in the United States" (reprint).

OSSERVATORE ROMANO, May 18, 1960, p. 1: *"Punti Fermi."*

OUR SUNDAY VISITOR, October 2, 1960, pp. 1, 4, 15: John F. Cronin, S.S., "Political Intolerance."

PERSPECTIVES, January-February, 1961, pp. 3–6: James J. Maguire, editorial.

PRESBYTERIAN JOURNAL (P.O. Box 2779, Asheville, N.C.): Dr. L. Nelson Bell, "Protestant Distinctives and the American Crisis" (reprint of the text of an address given at Montreat, N.C., August 21, 1960, and Washington, D.C., September 7, 1960).

PRESBYTERIAN LIFE, May 1, 1960, pp. 8–10: John Sutherland Bonnell, "Religion and the Presidency."

PRESBYTERIAN OUTLOOK, March 12, 1956, pp. 5–6: William Muehl, "The Christian in Politics."
October 3, 1960, pp. 5–7: Albert N. Wells, "Presidential Dilemma and Pastoral Concern."
October 31, 1960: "Before You Vote."

PROGRESSIVE, November, 1960, pp. 21–22: James MacGregor Burns, "The Religious Issue."

RECONSTRUCTIONIST, December 30, 1960, pp. 23–26: Stanley Rabinowitz, "Election Aftermath."

RELIGION IN LIFE, Spring, 1960, pp. 167–219: "Symposium on Approaches to Protestant-Roman Catholic Conversations."
pp. 167–178: George A. Barrois, "Roman Catholicism: New Look in Doctrine."
pp. 179–188: James Collins, "Philosophy in Catholic Life."
pp. 189–199: Thomas G. Sanders, "Some Themes of Modern Papal Political Thought."
pp. 200–210: Jaroslav Pelikan, "The Burden of Our Separation."

pp. 211–219: J. V. Langmead Casserley, "The Significance of the Liturgical Movement."

Summer, 1960, pp. 455–457: Maria F. Sulzback, "Protestants and Catholics in the U.S."

Winter, 1960–1961, pp. 17–31: Harry C. Spencer, "The Christian and Censorship of Television, Radio and Films."

pp. 32–37: Royal W. France, "Religious Freedom in the Atomic Age."

RELIGIOUS LIBERTY BULLETIN (pub. by National Council of the Churches of Christ in the U.S.A., Department of Religious Liberty), October 17, 1960, p. 1: "Religion and the Election."

RELIGIOUS NEWS SERVICE (43 West 57th St., New York 19, N.Y.). Daily news releases contained extensive coverage of religion and the campaign.

REPORTER, August 4, 1960, pp. 14–15: Max Ascoli, "From the Sports Arena."

October 13, 1960, pp. 30–32: Douglass Cater, "The Protestant Issue."

pp. 32–34: Rev. John W. Turnbull, "The Clergy Faces Mr. Kennedy."

pp. 34–36: James Q. Wilson, "How Will the Negroes Vote?"

October 27, 1960, pp. 26–27: Claire Sterling, "The Vatican and Kennedy."

November 10, 1960, pp. 10–11: "The Reporter's Notes."

January 19, 1961, pp. 32–33: Douglass Cater, "Puerto Rico: The Best Answer to Castro."

March 30, 1961, p. 12: "The Reporter's Notes."

REVUE DES SCIENCES PHILOSOPHIQUES ET THÉOLOGIQUES, XLI:4, pp. 601–631: Louis B. Geiger, "On Freedom" (reprinted in *Philosophy Today*, Fall, 1960, pp. 184–195).

ROUND TABLE, September, 1960, pp. 395–401: "U.S. of America: The Presidential Campaign."

SATURDAY REVIEW, October 31, 1959, p. 22: Elmo Roper, "The Myth of the Catholic Vote."

November 5, 1960, pp. 27, 53: Elmo Roper, "The Catholic Vote: A Second Look."

December 3, 1960, pp. 34, 64: Norman Cousins, "Sin and Political Freedom."

SIGN, July, 1960, pp. 11–14, 65: Most Rev. Karl J. Alter, "A Catholic President."

pp. 15–18: Jerome G. Kerwin, "Why This Fear of the Church?"

November, 1960, pp. 30–33: Thomas P. Neill, "American Unity and Religious Freedom."

SOCIAL ORDER, December, 1959, pp. 458–463: Francis Canavan, S.J., "Politics and Catholicism."

April, 1960, pp. 149–159: Donald R. Campion, S.J., "Catholicism and Ethnocentrism."

November, 1960, pp. 385–402: Edward Duff, S.J., "Church-State in the American Environment: An Historical and Legal Survey."

December, 1960, pp. 435–441: William L. Lucey, S.J., "The Election and After."

June, 1961, pp. 241–250: Robert F. Drinan, S.J., "Should the State Aid Private Schools?"

June, 1962, pp. 267–285: Patricia Barrett, "Religion and the 1960 Presidential Election."

SOCIAL PROGRESS (pub. by Board of Christian Education of the United Presbyterian Church in the U.S.A., Department of Social Education and Action), June, 1960, pp. 7 ff.: "A Symposium: Politics in This Election Year."

pp. 7–9: Murray S. Stedman, Jr., "In the Event That a Roman Catholic . . ."

pp. 13–16: William Lee Miller, "Party, Group, Philosophy Are the Issues."

Glenn L. Archer, "Everybody Should Know the Answer Now."

John C. Bennett, "It Would Depend."

TABLET, October 1, 1960: "The Presidential Campaign."
   October 15, 1960, pp. 932–933: "Laymen's Manifesto."
   November 5, 1960, pp. 1014–1015: "The Last Lap."
   November 19, 1960, pp. 1059–1060: "The American Presidency."
   p. 1076: "The Catholic Vote."

TEXAS OBSERVER, September 30, 1960 (special issue on religion and politics), pp. 1, 3: Ronnie Dugger, "Smith's Defense."
   pp. 1, 4: Ronnie Dugger, "Politicians in the Pulpit."

THEOLOGY TODAY, January, 1959, pp. 531–541: Antonio Márquez, "Catholic Controversy on Church and State."

TIME, September 19, 1960, pp. 21–22: "The Campaign: The Power of Negative Thinking."
   October 31, 1960, pp. 10–11: "Issues: Faces of Bigotry."
   pp. 11–12: "Fuss in Puerto Rico."
   November 7, 1960, pp. 22–23: "The Religion Question."
   November 16, 1960 (special issue): "The Election."

U.S. NEWS AND WORLD REPORT, August 1, 1960, pp. 68–72: "Catholic Vote: A Kennedy Staff Analysis."
   September 12, 1960, p. 94: "Campaign: Religion Becomes an Open Issue."
   September 19, 1960, pp. 96–97: "Latest on the 'Religious Issue': Text of a Statement by the National Conference of Citizens for Religious Freedom."
   September 26, 1960, pp. 74–81: "Both Sides of the 'Catholic Issue.' "
   October 10, 1960, p. 140: David Lawrence, "Gnawing Issue."
   October 24, 1960, pp. 66–67: E. Gressman, "Catholic Issue and the Supreme Court."
   December 5, 1960, pp. 77–78: "The Way the Vatican Views a Catholic in the White House."

UNIVERSITY OF CHICAGO LAW REVIEW, Autumn, 1961, pp. 2–96: Philip B. Kurland, "Of Church and State and the Supreme Court."

WALL STREET JOURNAL, September 12, 1960: Philip Geylin, "The Religious Issue: Anti-Catholicism Runs Deeper Than Expected, May Backfire on GOP."
September 21, 1960: "Who's Meddling?"

WESTERN POLITICAL QUARTERLY, March, 1961, Part 2: "The 1960 Elections in the West."
    pp. 287–299: Totton J. Anderson, "The Political West in 1960."
    pp. 309–326: Eugene C. Lee and William Buchanan, "The 1960 Election in California."
    pp. 327–330: Curtis Martin, "The 1960 Election in Colorado."
    pp. 373–382: Hugh A. Bone, "The 1960 Election in Washington."
    pp. 383–385: Herman H. Trachsel, "The 1960 Election in Wyoming."

WISEMAN REVIEW, Summer, 1961, pp. 99–108: Norman St.-John Stevas, "Catholicism and Religious Toleration."

WORD AND WAY, December 1, 1960, p. 4: H. H. McGinty, ed., "In a Strategic Position."

SERMONS, STATEMENTS, STUDIES, AND OTHER MATERIALS

AFL-CIO OFFICE FOR RELIGIOUS RELATIONS, "The Religious Issue in the 1960 Presidential Campaign" (16 mimeographed pages), New York, September 30, 1960. Memorandum containing reprints of significant articles.

AMERICAN JEWISH COMMITTEE, *The Committee Reporter,* October, 1960, pp. 6–7, 28: John Slawson, "The Bloc-Voting Myth."
Interreligious Newsletter, October, 1960, pp. 1–8: "Religion and the Presidency."

BAPTIST JOINT COMMITTEE ON PUBLIC AFFAIRS, Washington, D.C. *Report from the Capital: Religious Liberty, Baptist Principles, Public Affairs,* April, 1962, pp. 2–3: W. Barry

Garrett, "Third Temptation Sets Forth Church-State Problem."

p. 3: "Debate Continued on Financial Aid to Church Schools."

p. 8: "Religious Liberty Problems Erupt Around the World."

May, 1962, pp. 1, 3, 6: "U.S. Aid to Colombian Education Faces Religious Liberty Problems."

BENNETT, JOHN C., "The Religious Concern with Politics," New York, National Conference of Christians and Jews, 1960. First Morris Morgenstern Foundation Annual Award Lecture, New York, November 15, 1960.

BLUM, VIRGIL C., S.J., "State Monopoly in Higher Education" (6-page pamphlet), Knights of Columbus, 1960. Reprinted from *Columbia*, March, 1960.

BLUM, VIRGIL C., S.J., "The Right To Choose Your Own School," Missionary Society of St. Paul the Apostle of the State of New York, 1959. Reprinted from *Catholic World*, October, 1959, pp. 15–23.

CARLSON, C. EMANUEL, exec. dir., Baptist Joint Committee on Public Affairs, "Approaches to Our Public Relations Problems" (13 mimeographed pages). Address given at the Joint Promotion Conference of the Southern Baptist Convention, Nashville, September 21, 1960.

CONGREGATIONAL CHRISTIAN CONFERENCE OF NORTH DAKOTA, two-day workshop entitled "A Roman Catholic in Public Office," May 15–16, 1960. Leader: Dr. Hugo Thompson, professor of philosophy, Macalester College, St. Paul, Minn.

CONVERSE, PHILIP E., "Religion and Politics: The 1960 Elections." Paper given at the meeting of the American Sociological Association, St. Louis, August-September, 1961.

CRISWELL, REV. W. A., sermon, First Baptist Church, Dallas, Tex., July 3, 1960. (See "Religious Freedom, the Church, the State and Senator Kennedy" under "Campaign Pieces," above.)

145

DELAWARE VALLEY SEMINAR ON RELIGION AND THE FREE SOCIETY, entitled "The Nature of Religious Pluralism," 1959. Sponsored by the National Conference of Christians and Jews.

FAIR CAMPAIGN PRACTICES COMMITTEE, *Bulletin*, April, 1959.
Report, September, 1959, pp. 2–3: "Religion and Race."
Bulletin, November, 1959.
> April, 1960: "Special Report on Religion in the 1960 Campaign."
> November, 1960, p. 1: "Religious Issue Dwarfs Others."
> April, 1961, p. 6: "FCPC, Other Groups Map Special Campaign Post-Mortem."
Report, February, 1962: "The State-by-State Study of Smear: 1960."
Fair Play in Politics (pamphlet), New York, 1960.

FELKNOR, BRUCE L., "Bigotry in the Forthcoming Election Campaigns." Address given at the National Conference of Christians and Jews, Commission on Religious Organizations, Committee on Religious Liberty, New York, April 15, 1959.

FLANNERY, HARRY W., "Should a Roman Catholic Be Elected President?" Address.

GARRETT, W. BARRY, "Public Relations Problems for Southern Baptists in the National Election." Address given at the Joint Promotion Conference of the Southern Baptist Convention, Nashville, September 21, 1960.

GILBERT, RABBI ARTHUR, "A Catalogue of Church-State Problems" (8-page pamphlet), New York, Religious Education Association, 1962. Reprinted from *Religious Education*, November-December, 1961. Address given at the Annual Assembly, "Christian Social Progress," American Baptist Convention, Green Lake, Wis., August 23, 1960.

GILBERT, RABBI ARTHUR, "On the Subject of a Catholic for President" (14 mimeographed pages). Lecture.

KELLEY, DEAN M., "Questions of Church and State" (44-page pamphlet), 1960. Final report of the Research Consultation on Church and State undertaken by the Board of Social and

Economic Relations in the New York East Conference of the Methodist Church, 1957–1960.

NATIONAL CONFERENCE OF CHRISTIANS AND JEWS, New York, project entitled "Religious Freedom and Public Affairs," publishing a series of "Background Reports" designed to furnish news in depth on a specific situation that points up developments in a given area of religious freedom and public affairs.

NATIONAL COUNCIL OF THE CHURCHES OF CHRIST IN THE U.S.A., "Christian Responsibility in the 1960 Elections" (folder), New York, NCCC, February 25, 1960. A resolution adopted by the General Board of the NCCC.

O'BRIEN, REV. JOHN A., "And Justice for All: Federal Aid and the Non-Public School" (28-page pamphlet), Washington, National Council of Catholic Men and National Catholic Welfare Conference, Education Department.

POWELL, THEODORE, "A Plea for a Different Climate." Address given at the Regional Convention of the American Association of School Administrators, Philadelphia, March 28, 1961.

REPUBLICAN NATIONAL COMMITTEE, Research Staff, "The 1960 Elections: A Summary Report," 2nd rev. prtg. (61 mimeographed pages), Washington, April, 1961.

SHAW, RUSSELL, "The Parental Right to Education" (pamphlet), Washington, National Council of Catholic Men and National Catholic Welfare Conference, Education Department.

SHAW, RUSSELL, "Fifty Questions and Answers on Federal Aid to Education and Related Matters," Washington, National Council of Catholic Men and National Catholic Welfare Conference, Education Department.

"A STATEMENT ON RELIGIOUS LIBERTY BY AMERICAN CATHOLIC LAYMEN," October, 1960. (See Appendix B.)

SYNAGOGUE COUNCIL OF AMERICA, "Safeguarding Religious Liberty: Statements of Policy and Position on Religion and Public Education and Other Aspects of Church-State Relationships" (pamphlet), New York, Synagogue Council of Amer-

147

ica and National Community Relations Advisory Council, December, 1957.

WEIGEL, GUSTAVE, S.J., "A Theological Consideration of the Relations Between Church and State." Sermon given at the Shrine of the Most Blessed Sacrament, Washington, D.C., September 27, 1960.

APPENDIX B

Policy Statements

A STATEMENT BY THE NATIONAL CONFERENCE OF CITIZENS FOR RELIGIOUS FREEDOM, WASHINGTON, D.C., SEPTEMBER 7, 1960

DESPITE efforts to ignore or stifle it, the religious issue remains a major factor in the current political campaign. Indeed, it has become one of the most significant issues. We of this conference, ministers and laymen in Protestant churches of 37 denominations, realize that the candidacy of a Roman Catholic for President of the United States has aroused questions which must be faced frankly by the American people.

We believe that this religious issue should be handled with utmost discretion; that it should be discussed only in a spirit of truth, tolerance and fairness, and that no persons should engage in hate-mongering, bigotry, prejudice or unfounded charges. We further believe that persons who are of the Roman Catholic faith can be just as honest, patriotic and public-spirited as those of any other faith. We believe in the same freedom of religion for Roman Catholics as for ourselves and all other people.

The key question is whether it is in the best interest of our society for any church organization to attempt to exercise control over its members in political and civic affairs. While the current Roman Catholic contender for the Presidency states specifically that he would not be so influenced, his Church insists that he is duty-

SOURCE: *U.S. News and World Report,* September 19, 1960, pp. 96–97. The text of this and other statements in Appendix B can be found in many other sources.

bound to submit to its direction. This unresolved conflict leaves doubt in the minds of millions of our citizens.

1. The Roman Catholic Church is a political as well as a religious organization. Traditionally, its hierarchy has assumed and exercised temporal power, unless and until that power has been successfully checked by the instruments of representative government. Today the Vatican in Rome, representing the seat of Catholic religious and temporal power, maintains diplomatic relations with the governments of 42 countries, exchanging ambassadors who have official status. Spokesmen for the Vatican in the United States have repeatedly urged establishment of diplomatic relations with the Roman Catholic Church, including appointment by the President of an official representative.

The President has the responsibility in our Government for conducting foreign relations, including receiving and appointing ambassadors. It is inconceivable that a Roman Catholic President would not be under extreme pressure by the hierarchy of his Church to accede to its policies with respect to foreign relations in matters including representation to the Vatican.

2. The Roman Catholic Church has specifically repudiated on many occasions the principle sacred to us that every man shall be free to follow the dictates of his conscience in religious matters. Such pronouncements are, furthermore, set forth as required beliefs for every Roman Catholic, including the Democratic nominee. Binding upon him, as upon all members of this Church, is the belief that Protestant faiths are heretical and counterfeit and that they have no theoretical right to exist.

3. The record of the Roman Catholic Church in many countries where it is predominant is one of denial of equal rights for all of other faiths. The constitutions of a number of countries prohibit any persons except Roman Catholics from serving as President or chief of state.

The laws of most predominantly Catholic countries extend to Catholics privileges not permitted to those of other faiths.

In countries such as Spain and Colombia, Protestant ministers

150

and religious workers have been arrested, imprisoned and otherwish persecuted because of their religion. No Protestant church or Jewish synagogue can be marked as such on its exterior.

4. We realize that many American Catholics would disagree with the policies of their Church in other countries and would not want to introduce them here under any circumstances. But this does not altogether reassure us.

The Roman Catholic Church in the United States has repeatedly attempted to break down the wall of separation of church and state by a continuous campaign to secure public funds for the support of its schools and other institutions. In various areas where they predominate, Catholics have seized control of the public schools, staffed them with nun teachers wearing their Church garb, and introduced the catechism and practices of their Church.

In Ohio today—a State with a Roman Catholic Governor—according to an Attorney General's ruling, Roman Catholic nuns and sisters may be placed on the public payroll as schoolteachers.

The record shows that one of the bills introduced by John F. Kennedy—HR 5838, 81st Congress—now a nominee for the Presidency, as a member of the House of Representatives from Massachusetts, had as its purpose federal aid to education which included private and parochial schools. Representative Kennedy also sought to amend the Barden bill in the 81st Congress in such a way as to provide funds for parochial schools. He was, however, the only Senator of Roman Catholic faith who voted against the Morse amendment to the Aid-to-Education Act in the 86th Congress in 1960. The Morse amendment would have provided partial grants and partial loans for the construction of parochial schools. We are hopeful that the newer phase of Senator Kennedy's thinking on this issue will prevail, but we can only measure the new against the old.

By recommendation, persuasion and veto power, the President can and must shape the course of legislation in this country. Is it reasonable to assume that a Roman Catholic President would be able to withstand altogether the determined efforts of the hier-

151

archy of his Church to gain further funds and favors for its schools and institutions, and otherwise breach the wall of separation of church and state?

5. Under the canon law of the Roman Catholic Church, a President of this faith would not be allowed to participate in interfaith meetings; he could not worship in a Protestant church without securing the permission of an ecclesiastic. Would not a Roman Catholic President thus be gravely handicapped in offering to the American people and to the world an example of the religious liberty our people cherish?

Brotherhood in a pluralistic society like ours depends on a firm wall of separation between church and state. We feel that the American hierarchy of the Roman Catholic Church can only increase religious tensions and political-religious problems by attempting to break down this wall. Much depends upon strong support for this well-tested wall of separation by Americans of all faiths.

Finally, that there is a "religious issue" in the present political campaign is not the fault of any candidate. It is created by the nature of the Roman Catholic Church which is, in a very real sense, both a church and also a temporal state.

A STATEMENT ON RELIGIOUS LIBERTY IN RELATION TO THE 1960 NATIONAL CAMPAIGN

Foreword

ONE HUNDRED churchmen and scholars—Protestant, Greek Orthodox, Roman Catholic, Jewish—sponsored this statement, released September 12, 1960, and widely publicized in newspapers and other periodicals. This printing in leaflet form is designed to further its usefulness. Distribution in draft form began on September second. Some recipients absent from home when the draft arrived have authorized inclusion of their names since release to the press.

SOURCE: Printed leaflet dated September, 1960.

The sponsors signed solely as individuals, without reference to any official affiliations. The statement has also been drawn without reference to any political party or party philosophy.

Its sole purpose is to attempt to bring basic American principles of religious liberty in a democracy into a dispassionate focus, so that all citizens, irrespective of their religious affiliations, may function reasonably and with foresight in an area that too often lends itself to emotion.

While each of the signatories has acted as an individual, they are all drawn together by a principle that is best described by a sentence in the statement itself. The sentence reads, "The judgment of God finds us at a particular moment in history, confronted by its unique challenges and dilemmas, and it is here that our testing is."

The Statement

We reaffirm our loyalty to the Constitution of the United States and its provision that "no religious test shall ever be required as a qualification to any office or public trust under the United States," and the declaration in the American Bill of Rights that "Congress shall make no law respecting an establishment of religion or prohibiting the free exercise thereof."

We affirm that religious liberty is basic, both historically and philosophically, to all our liberties, and that religious and civil liberties are interdependent and indivisible.

It is our conviction that man's freedom is an essential attribute of human nature. The sacredness of this truth has long been recognized as fundamental to Western society. The founders of this nation, in emancipating themselves from tyranny, asserted their right to life, to liberty, and to the pursuit of happiness.

These rights are guaranteed in our Constitution to each of us as citizens, and also to the association, societies, and religious faiths to which we belong. Freedom is fundamental to faith. Freedom is fundamental to the exercise of conscience. It is necessary, therefore, to the essence of our faith that we respect the diversity of religious viewpoints and their freedoms.

153

Unique Challenges

We believe that it is the responsibility of the members of various religious organizations to oppose vigorously all attempts to make religious affiliation the basis of the voter's choice of candidates for public office. It is a vicious practice and repugnant to all honorable Americans to set class against class, race against race, and religion against religion.

The judgment of God finds us at a particular moment in history, confronted by its unique challenges and dilemmas, and it is there that our testing is. In the circumstances that now confront us, we must act according to our principles, or be found wanting. In the election campaign of 1960 we face a real and inescapable challenge with respect to the relation between a man's religion and the responsibility of the nation's highest elective office.

To speak in this immediate situation will occasion charges of partisanship, but we cannot be silent. We are anxious only that the voter's choice be made on true and vital grounds and issues, on the candidates' whole character and record, and not solely or primarily upon the matter of religious affiliation.

It is our determination and our duty to clarify this issue in order that votes shall not be cast for one candidate or the other because of religious prejudice or misinformation.

More serious by far than all real or fancied risks is the damage that most certainly will be done to our American community if 40,000,000 of our fellow-citizens should be made to feel that they are barred from full and free participation in our national life because of their religious affiliation!

Guidelines Proposed

That we may further the fulfillment of our American democracy under God, we suggest that the foregoing affirmations and the following principles be guidelines for action in the 1960 election.

1. The exclusion of members of any family of faith from public office on the basis of religious affiliation violates the fundamental

conditions of a free democratic society, as expressed in the spirit of our Constitution.

There must be no second-class citizenship in the United States, whether it be based on religion, race, class, or national origin.

2. The religious faith of a public officer is relevant to the conduct of his office.

The religious faith of a person of integrity will influence his private and his public conduct. The relevance of faith to his personal spiritual life is a private matter. His religious faith can give him an insight, independence, and composure that will enable him to make dispassionate judgments in the crises of public life, and lead the nation to a more creative fulfillment of its destiny.

The bearing of the religious views of any candidate of any party upon his decisions in public office is a public matter. Inquiry regarding this relevancy is an exercise of responsible citizenship, if conducted in such a way as not to violate the constitutional prohibition against any religious test for public office.

3. No citizen in public office dare be false either to his conscience or to his oath of office.

Both his conscience and his oath impose responsibilities sacred under the law of God. If he cannot reconcile the responsibilities entailed by his oath with his conscience, then he must resign, lest he fail his nation and his God.

4. The fact that a major religious group has so far never furnished the nation with a candidate who won election to a particular public office does not obligate the voters to elect a candidate of that faith to that office solely to demonstrate our devotion to democracy.

This would establish a religious test for public office much narrower than the one complained of, and contrary to the obvious intent of the Constitution. It would, furthermore, focus attention on a marginal qualification rather than on the essential qualities of personal integrity, leadership capacity, and policies relating to central issues.

155

5. No religious organization should seek to influence and dominate public officials for its own institutional advantage.

The exercise of public office must always be in the public interest, and serve the welfare of the whole community, local or national. The rights and liberties of each and every voluntary association must be respected and protected as long as they do not infringe upon the like rights of others.

Full Liberty Advocated

6. Every person of every faith must be accorded full religious liberty, and no person should be coerced into accepting any religious belief or practice. No religious group should be given special preference or advantage by the state, nor allowed to use state agencies for the restriction of other faiths.

7. A candidate's faith, and his affirmations of it, as they bear upon his responsibilities in public office, should be viewed in their best light rather than their worst, and the response and expectation of the nation should be such as will encourage him to attain the highest spiritual and moral realization which his own faith can inspire.

8. Just as the choice of candidates for public office should be based upon integrity, leadership, and convictions on basic issues, so the public officer after his election is obligated to make his appointments to subordinate positions on a non-discriminatory basis, using competence and record rather than religious affiliation as the criteria of selection.

9. The President's participation in important national and community religious functions can be a fine symbol of the common concern for the spiritual welfare of the nation. But if for reasons of his own he feels that participation in a particular religious ceremony is not in order, it would be contrary to the civic character of the American Presidency for him to feel obligated to accept the invitation.

Participation in special religious ceremonials is an aspect of the

Presidency that is secondary in importance to matters of constitutional responsibility, such as the conduct of foreign affairs, the governing of the nation, and the execution of the laws, and it must be weighed in proportion to these functions in any estimate of a candidate's suitability for that office.

10. Every public official who is a member of a religious group should, of course, take into consideration the spiritual and moral principles of his faith in confronting decisions he must make. But in our pluralistic society he will recognize that the values in historic faiths other than his own must be brought to bear upon the problems of the day. He alone, under the judgment of God, can fully appraise the force and applicability of all such values and advice for his situation, and he should seek to apply all in such a way as to enhance and undergird the best interests of the nation.

Following is the list of the 100 persons who signed the statement. They include fifty-five Protestants, twenty-nine Roman Catholics, one Greek Orthodox and fifteen of the Jewish faith.

The Rev. Dr. Hampton Adams, New York

Rabbi Morris Adler, Detroit

The Rev. Dr. Forest Ashbrook, Scarsdale, N.Y.

Rabbi Bernard Bamberger, New York

The Rev. Prof. John C. Bennett, New York

Herbert Berman, Queens, N.Y.

Dr. Harry J. Carman, New York

The Rev. Dr. Samuel McCrea Cavert, Bronxville, N.Y.

Porter Chandler, New York

Wayne H. Cowan, New York, managing editor, *Christianity and Crisis*

The Rev. Dr. Clarence W. Cranford, Washington

Richard Cardinal Cushing, Archbishop of Boston

The Rev. Thurston N. Davis, S.J., editor in chief, *America*, New York

Cleveland E. Dodge, New York

Prof. Dan W. Dodson, New York University

The Right Rev. Horace W. B. Donegan, Protestant Episcopal Bishop of New York

The Rev. Robert F. Drinan,

157

S.J., dean, Boston College Law School

The Right Rev. Angus Dun, Washington

The Most Rev. Robert J. Dwyer, Bishop of Reno

The Right Rev. Richard Emrich, Detroit

Rabbi Maurice N. Eisendrath, New York

Moses I. Feuerstein, Brookline, Mass.

Dr. George Forell, Maywood, Ill.

The Very Rev. Msgr. Timothy J. Flynn, New York

Dr. Herbert Grezork, Newton Center, Mass.

The Rev. Dr. Gerard R. Gnade, Ridgewood, N.J.

Miss Dorothy I. Haight, New York

Francis Stuart Harmon, New York

Carlton J. H. Hayes, New York

Rabbi Arthur Hertzberg, Englewood, N.J.

Miss Jane M. Hoey, New York

The Rev. Dr. James E. Hoffman, Hasbrouck Heights, N.J.

Prof. William E. Hocking, Madison, N.H.

The Rev. Luther Holcomb, Dallas

Paul Horgan, Roswell, N.M.

Mrs. Mildred McAfee Horton, Randolph, N.H.

The Rev. Dr. Fred Hoskins, New York

Paul Hume, Washington

George K. Hunton, New York

Archbishop Iakovos, New York

Rabbi Jay Kaufman, New York

Rabbi Wolfe Kelman, New York

Prof. Jerome G. Kerwin, University of Chicago

Rabbi Israel Klavan, Queens, N.Y.

The Rev. Dr. J. H. Jackson, Chicago

The Rev. Dr. F. Ernest Johnson, New York

Prof. Harry W. Jones, Columbia University, New York

Dr. Lewis Webster Jones, New York

The Rev. John La Farge, S.J., New York

Dr. Charles R. Lawrence, Pomona, N.Y.

Morris Laub, New York

The Rev. Dr. J. Oscar Lee, Brooklyn

Miss Edith Lerrigo, New York

The Right Rev. Arthur Lichtenberger, Greenwich, Conn.

The Most Rev. Robert E. Lucey, Archbishop of San Antonio, Tex.

William C. Martin, Methodist Bishop of Dallas, Tex.

Benjamin E. Mays, president, Morehouse College, Atlanta

The Rev. Dr. O. C. Maxwell, New York

Dr. Millicent McIntosh, president, Barnard College, New York

Francis E. McMahon, Chicago

Mrs. Eugene Meyer, Mt. Kisco, N.Y.

Joseph J. Morrow, Stamford, Conn.

The Rev. Dr. Arthur L. Miller, Denver

The Right Rev. Msgr. Edward G. Murray, S.T.D., Roslindale, Mass.

The Rev. John Courtney Murray, S.J., Woodstock College, Md.

The Rev. Claud D. Nelson, New York

The Rev. Prof. John Oliver Nelson, New Haven

The Rev. Dr. Reinhold Niebuhr, New York

Bishop G. Bromley Oxnam, Scarsdale, N.Y.

The Right Rev. James A. Pike, Protestant Episcopal Bishop, Diocese of California, San Francisco

The Rev. Dr. Liston Pope, New Haven

The Rev. Dr. F. W. Price, New York

Mrs. Roger Putnam, Springfield, Mass.

Rabbi Sidney L. Regner, New Rochelle, N.Y.

Prof. Ira De A. Reid, Haverford, Pa.

The Rev. Dr. Frederick E. Reissig, Washington

The Rev. J. H. Robinson, New York

Rabbi William F. Rosenblum, New York

Rabbi Edward T. Sandrow, Cedarhurst, Long Island

The Very Rev. Francis B. Sayre, Washington

The Right Rev. Henry Knox Sherrill, Boxford, Mass.

Gerard E. Sherry, Monterey, Calif.

Dr. George N. Shuster, New Rochelle, N.Y.

Mrs. Harper Sibley, Rochester, N.Y.

Edward Skillin, editor, *The Commonweal,* New York

Harold C. Stevens, New York

Miss Thelma Stevens, New York

Chauncey Stillman, New York

Dr. Donald C. Stone, Pittsburgh

Mrs. Wallace Streeter, Washington

John B. Sullivan, New York

159

Dr. Channing H. Tobias, New York

James F. Twohy, San Jose, Calif.

Schuyler N. Warren, New York

The Rev. Dr. Luther A. Weigle, New Haven

Rabbi Charles Weinberg, Malden, Mass.

Dr. Samson R. Weiss, New York

Bishop Lloyd C. Wicke, New York

Paul D. Williams, Richmond, Va.

Dr. Jesse R. Wilson, Wells, Tex.

And the following additional persons:

Dr. Merriman Cunningim, St. Louis, Mo.

Prof. Bernard Lander, New York University

Rev. Dr. Carlyle Marney, Charlotte

Herbert P. Lansdale, New York

Rt. Rev. Jonathan G. Sherman, Garden City, L.I., N.Y.

Bishop W. J. Walls, Yonkers, N.Y.

Rev. Dr. A. Dudley Ward, Chicago

TEXT OF SENATOR JOHN F. KENNEDY'S SPEECH TO THE GREATER HOUSTON MINISTERIAL ASSOCIATION, SEPTEMBER 12, 1960

I AM GRATEFUL for your generous invitation to state my views.

While the so-called religious issue is necessarily and properly the chief topic here tonight, I want to emphasize from the outset that we have far more critical issues to face in the 1960 election: The spread of Communist influence, until it now festers 90 miles off the coast of Florida—the humiliating treatment of our President and Vice President by those who no longer respect our power—the hungry children I saw in West Virginia, the old people who cannot pay their doctor bills, the families forced to give up their farms—an America with too many slums, with too few schools, and too late to the moon and outer space.

SOURCE: *St. Louis Post-Dispatch*, September 13, 1960, p. 7a.

These are the real issues which should decide this campaign. And they are not religious issues—for war and hunger and ignorance and despair know no religious barriers.

But because I am a Catholic, and no Catholic has ever been elected President, the real issues in this campaign have been obscured—perhaps deliberately, in some quarters less responsible than this. So it is apparently necessary for me to state once again—not what kind of church I believe in, for that should be important only to me—but what kind of America I believe in.

I believe in an America where the separation of church and state is absolute—where no Catholic prelate would tell the President (should he be Catholic) how to act, and no Protestant minister would tell his parishioners for whom to vote—where no church or church school is granted any public funds or political preference—and where no man is denied public office merely because his religion differs from the President who might appoint him or the people who might elect him.

I believe in an America that is officially neither Catholic, Protestant nor Jewish—where no public official either requests or accepts instructions on public policy from the Pope, the National Council of Churches or any other ecclesiastical source—where no religious body seeks to impose its will directly or indirectly upon the general populace or the public acts of its officials—and where religious liberty is so indivisible that an act against one church is treated as an act against all.

For, while this year it may be a Catholic against whom the finger of suspicion is pointed, in other years it has been, and may someday be again, a Jew—or a Quaker—or a Unitarian—or a Baptist. It was Virginia's harassment of Baptist preachers, for example, that helped lead to Jefferson's statute of religious freedom. Today I may be the victim—but tomorrow it may be you—until the whole fabric of our harmonious society is ripped at a time of great national peril.

Finally, I believe in an America where religious intolerance will some day end—where all men and all churches are treated as equal—where every man has the same right to attend or not attend

161

the church of his choice—where there is no Catholic vote, no anti-Catholic vote, no bloc voting of any kind—and where Catholics, Protestants and Jews, at both the lay and pastoral level, will refrain from those attitudes of disdain and division which have so often marred their works in the past, and promote instead the American ideal of brotherhood.

That is the kind of America in which I believe, and it represents the kind of presidency in which I believe—a great office that must neither be humbled by making it the instrument of any one religious group, nor tarnished by arbitrarily withholding its occupancy from the members of any one religious group. I believe in a President whose religious views are his own private affair, neither imposed by him upon the nation or imposed by the nation upon him as a condition to holding that office.

I would not look with favor upon a President working to subvert the First Amendment's guarantees of religious liberty. Nor would our system of checks and balances permit him to do so—and neither do I look with favor upon those who would work to subvert Article VI of the Constitution by requiring a religious test—even by indirection—for it. If they disagree with that safeguard, they should be out openly working to repeal it.

I want a chief executive whose public acts are responsible to all groups and obligated to none—who can attend any ceremony, service or dinner his office may appropriately require of him—and whose fulfillment of his presidential oath is not limited or conditioned by any religious oath, ritual or obligation.

This is the kind of America I believe in—and this is the kind I fought for in the South Pacific, and the kind my brother died for in Europe. No one suggested then that we might have a "divided loyalty," that we did "not believe in liberty" or that we belonged to a disloyal group that threatened the "freedoms for which our forefathers died."

And in fact this is the kind of America for which our forefathers died—when they fled here to escape religious test oaths that denied office to members of less favored churches—when they fought for the Constitution, the Bill of Rights, and the Virginia

Statute of Religious Freedom—and when they fought at the shrine I visited today, the Alamo. For side by side with Bowie and Crockett died McCafferty and Bailey and Carey—but no one knows whether they were Catholics or not. For there was no religious test at the Alamo.

I ask you tonight to follow in that tradition—to judge me on the basis of my record of 14 years in Congress—on my declared stands against an ambassador to the Vatican, against unconstitutional aid to parochial schools, and against any boycott of the public schools (which I have attended myself)—instead of judging me on the basis of these pamphlets and publications we all have seen that carefully select quotations out of context from the statements of Catholic church leaders, usually in other countries, frequently in other centuries and rarely relevant to any situation here—and always omitting, of course, the statement of the American Bishops in 1948 which strongly endorsed church-state separation, and which more nearly reflects the views of almost every American Catholic. I do not consider these other quotations binding upon my public acts—why should you? But let me say with respect to other countries, that I am wholly opposed to the state being used by any religious group, Catholic or Protestant, to compel, prohibit or persecute the free exercise of any other religion. And I hope that you and I condemn with equal fervor those nations which deny their presidency to Protestants and those which deny it to Catholics. And rather than cite the misdeeds of those who differ, I would cite the record of the Catholic Church in such nations as Ireland and France—and the independence of such statesmen as Adenauer and De Gaulle.

But let me stress again that these are my views—for, contrary to common newspaper usage, I am not the Catholic candidate for President. I am the Democratic party's candidate for President, who happens also to be a Catholic. I do not speak for my church on public matters—and the church does not speak for me.

Whatever issue may come before me as President—on birth control, divorce, censorship, gambling, or any other subject—I will make my decision in accordance with these views, in accordance

163

with what my conscience tells me to be the national interest, and without regard to outside religious pressures or dictates. And no power or threat of punishment could cause me to decide otherwise.

But if the time should ever come—and I do not concede any conflict to be even remotely possible—when my office would require me to either violate my conscience or violate the national interest, then I would resign the office; and I hope any conscientious public servant would do the same.

But I do not intend to apologize for these views to my critics of either Catholic or Protestant faith—nor do I intend to disavow either my views or my church in order to win this election. If I should lose on the real issues, I shall return to my seat in the Senate, satisfied that I had tried my best and was fairly judged. But if this election is decided on the basis that 40,000,000 Americans lost their chance of being President on the day they were baptized, then it is the whole nation that will be the loser, in the eyes of Catholics and non-Catholics around the world, in the eyes of history, and in the eyes of our own people.

But if, on the other hand, I should win the election, then I shall devote every effort of mind and spirit to fulfilling the oath of the presidency—practically identical, I might add, to the oath I have taken for 14 years in the Congress. For, without reservation, I can "solemnly swear that I will faithfully execute the office of President of the United States, and will to the best of my ability preserve, protect and defend the Constitution . . . so help me God."

A STATEMENT ON RELIGIOUS LIBERTY BY AMERICAN CATHOLIC LAYMEN

October, 1960.

THE PRESENT controversy about the Catholic Church and the Presidency proves once again that large numbers of our fellow-citizens seriously doubt the commitment of Catholics to the principles of a free society. This fact creates problems which extend

SOURCE: Mimeographed sheets dated October, 1960.

164

far beyond this year's elections and threaten to make permanent, bitter divisions in our national life. Such a result would obviously be tragic from the standpoints both of religious tolerance and of civic peace.

In order to avert this, we ask all Americans to examine (more carefully, perhaps, than they have in the past) the relationship between religious conscience and civil society. We think that, in the present situation, Catholics especially are obliged to make their position clear.

There is much bigotry abroad in the land, some of it masquerading under the name of "freedom." There is also genuine concern. To the extent that many Catholics have failed to make known their devotion to religious liberty for all, to the extent that they at times have appeared to seek sectarian advantage, we must admit that we have contributed to doubts about our intentions. It is our hope that this statement may help to dispel such doubts.

To this end we make the following declarations of our convictions about religion and the free society. We do this with an uncompromised and uncompromising loyalty both to the Catholic Church and to the American Republic.

1. We believe in the freedom of the religious conscience and in the Catholic's obligation to guarantee full freedom of belief and worship as a civil right. This obligation follows from basic Christian convictions about the dignity of the human person and the inviolability of the individual conscience. And we believe that Catholics have a special duty to work for the realization of the principle of freedom of religion in every nation, whether they are a minority or a majority of the citizens.

2. We deplore the denial of religious freedom in any land. We especially deplore this denial in countries where Catholics constitute a majority—even an overwhelming majority. In the words of Giacomo Cardinal Lercaro, the present Archbishop of Bologna: "Christian teaching concerning the presence of God in the human soul and belief in the transcendent value in history of the human person lays the foundation for use of persuasive methods in mat-

ters of religious faith and forbids coercion and violence." The Catholic's commitment to religious liberty, therefore, he says, "is not a concession suggested by prudence and grudgingly made to the spirit of the times." Rather, it is rooted "in the permanent principles of Catholicism."

3. We believe constitutional separation of church and state offers the best guarantee both of religious freedom and of civic peace. The principle of separation is part of our American heritage, and as citizens who are Catholics we value it as an integral part of our national life. Efforts which tend to undermine the principle of separation, whether they come from Catholics, Protestants or Jews, believers or unbelievers, should be resisted no matter how well-intentioned such efforts might be.

4. We believe that among the fundamentals of religious liberty are the freedom of the church to teach its members and the freedom of its members to accept the teachings of their church. These freedoms should be invulnerable to the pressures of conformity. For civil society to dictate how a citizen forms his conscience would be a gross violation of freedom. Civil society's legitimate interest is limited to the public acts of the believer as they affect the whole community.

5. In his public acts as they affect the whole community the Catholic is bound in conscience to promote the common good and to avoid any seeking of a merely sectarian advantage. He is bound also to recognize the proper scope of independence of the political order. As Jacques Maritain has pointed out, the Church provides Catholics with certain general principles to guide us in our life as citizens. It directs us to the pursuit of justice and the promotion of the common good in our attitudes toward both domestic and international problems. But it is as individual citizens and officeholders, not as a religious bloc, that we make the specific application of these principles in political life. Here we function not as "Catholic citizens" but as citizens who are Catholics. It is in this spirit that we submit this statement to our fellow Americans.